BUILD A BUSINESS THAT ~~CAN BE SOLD, EVEN~~ IF YOU HAVE NO INTENTION OF SELLING.

THE
Aloha
MONEY
MACHINE

9 Steps For Creating A Business Money-Making Machine

Murf Murphy

With a foreword by Mark LeBlanc, author of *Growing Your Business*

INDIE BOOKS
INTERNATIONAL

No part of this publication may be reproduced or distributed in any form or by any means without the prior permission of the publisher. Requests for permission should be directed to permissions@ indiebooksintl.com, or mailed to Permissions, Indie Books International, 2424 Vista Way, Suite 316, Oceanside, CA 92054.

The views and opinions in this book are those of the author at the time of writing this book, and do not reflect the opinions of Indie Books International or its editors.

Neither the publisher nor the author is engaged in rendering legal, tax or other professional services through this book. The information is for business education purposes only. If expert assistance is required, the services of appropriate professionals should be sought. The publisher and the author shall have neither liability nor responsibility to any person or entity with respect to any loss or damage caused directly or indirectly by the information in this publication.

ISBN: 978-1-947480-88-9
Library of Congress Control Number: 2019919272

Library of Congress notation about George W. Murphy

The Aloha Money Machine Method™ is a pending trademark of Corey Murphy

Thank you to *Hawaii Business Magazine* for providing the archival photos on page 40 and 125.

Photos on page 79 and 82 courtesy of the *Honolulu Star-Advertiser*.

Designed by Joni McPherson, mcphersongraphics.com

INDIE BOOKS INTERNATIONAL, LLC
2424 VISTA WAY, SUITE 316
OCEANSIDE, CA 92054

www.indiebooksintl.com

Contents

Foreword v

Preface vii

Part I Why Create A Money-Making Machine 1

   1   Why Most Business Owners Can't Sell Their Business 3

   2   The Solution: Create Your Aloha Money Machine 11

Part II The Aloha Money Machine Method 37

   3   Step One: Focus On The End 39

   4   Step Two: Follow The Money 47

   5   Step Three: Attract Customers 53

   6   Step Four: Craft Your Story 59

   7   Step Five: Build The System 65

   8   Step Six: Hire Right 73

   9   Step Seven: Networking Your Database 83

  10 Step Eight: Manage The System 87

  11 Step Nine: Highest And Best Use of Time 93

Part III Selling the Aloha Money Machine 103

  12 The Next Step 105

Epilogue 119

Afterword 127

Appendix A Acknowledgments 129

Appendix B About The Author 131

Works Referenced 133

Dedicated to
the memory of
George W. Murphy

*To the ones who seek a safe and secure
harbor: I hope that they may experience
secondhand the excitement
of the unknown sea
through blind faith.*

Foreword

In your hands you hold a book that can make a difference in how you think and take action in your business. Whether you are in the early stages of developing your business or you have been in business for some time, you will find principles and practices that will guide and shape your next chapter of success.

When I first met Murf, I found him to be smart, thoughtful, and incredibly committed to helping others achieve success. The lessons he has learned along the way are street smart, sound, and proven to work time and time again.

You would do well to keep this book handy and refer to it often. It will be a lighthouse guide in directing your decisions, actions, and activities in helping you become as successful as you are capable of becoming.

Successful entrepreneurs today combine the best in strategy, ideas, and spirit. Murf has done an admirable job in all three elements. I hope you have an opportunity to meet Murf, hear him speak, and even possibly hire him to be your business coach. You will be glad you did.

Best,

Mark LeBlanc, CSP
Author of *Never Be the Same, Build Your Consulting Practice* and *Defining YOU*

Preface

This book is about how to build a business into a consistent money machine that can survive without you. (Caution: You might not want to tell anyone that you're building a business that can survive without you, or you may have to hire someone to start your car and taste your food.) Once you're able to grow your business into a money machine, you will experience something that only a few will ever experience.

For many of us, growing a business into a money machine could be the very best shot at a comfortable retirement or becoming rich. My goal was to write an entertaining business book to give you examples from real people who have built their own money machines and created their own success by focusing on the future of their businesses. Learn from the past, live in the present, focus on the end.

I could have written a book filled with facts and figures, but that would be a lot of work and who needs that. Kidding. I didn't fill this book with facts and figures because I believe that stories are more powerful than spreadsheets. There's a reason that the Brothers Grimm never wrote a fairy tale called "Hansel and the Accountant." As humans, we are hardwired to learn from stories, and what better way to learn? The Aloha Money Machine is the story of one such man who achieved success repeatedly in Hawaii. He was my inspiration for writing this book and to become financially free.

I hope that this book will provide some focus and clarity to business owners and those thinking of opening a business, and maybe provide some valuable advice or new strategies along the way.

My life's work has taken me around the world in search of financial success. I've met with thousands of business owners, and although I thought most had compelling stories, most were not financially free and did not have the insight to build a truly successful business themselves. Anyone can start a business. The trick is growing one that you can sell, if you choose to.

The people who have achieved business success themselves are the great inspirations in my own life. One such person who has impacted my life was named Hawaii's businessman of the year in 1965, long before I was born.

Aloha,

Corey "Murf" Murphy
Oceanside, CA
August 2019

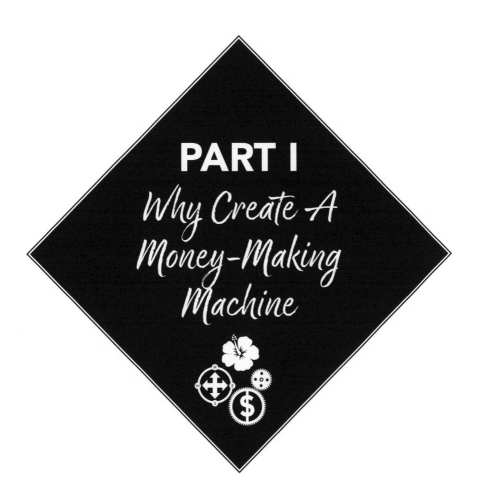

PART I
Why Create A Money-Making Machine

1

Why Most Business Owners Can't Sell Their Business

Although I might not know your specific business, I do know your business better than you think. And though my mother often admonished me to "mind my *own* business," I firmly believe that I can help you with yours. Sorry, Mom.

Whether you're a start-up, a not-for-profit, or in a business to make millions, the survival of your business revolves around money. In one way or another, we are all connected to money. Money is the glue that holds all business together and will be the main factor for your success in business. And while money will not always give happiness, it can buy something so close to happiness that you can't tell the difference. Seriously, money may not give you happiness, but it will give you the freedom to do the work you love, versus doing the work you have to do.

I remember getting a phone call late one Monday evening that would change my focus from making short-term money to long-term wealth. The caller on the other end of the line simply asked, "Have you ever heard of Amway?" Kidding, of course—he really said, "Quit what you're doing, Murf, and come work for me. I'm making $50,000 a month; you've got to work for me."

My first thought was, he's either selling drugs, or high on drugs, because nobody makes that kind of money legally. I was wrong.

The man on the phone was a friend who was making that much a month in commissions as a mortgage broker in 2007. My friend was an independent contractor who was building a team of salespeople and wanted to hire me on the spot. Although I was making consistent one-off sales, I wasn't yet making $50,000 a month, and the idea of closing my business to go to work for him was extremely tempting.

To make matters worse, I was having a hard time in my own small business. My best employee of five years had just given notice to quit, and my second-best employee was now threating to walk as well. As the owner of the business, I was so discouraged I was thinking about firing myself.

Being an owner of a small business was tough, and I thought seriously about shutting down my business for good. It would have been easy for me to walk away, as I didn't have partners, and my best employees had one foot out the door anyway.

But I didn't shut down the business, as I knew that I was growing something more than just a one-time sale. I would eventually grow a business into an asset. In the end, this would turn out to be the best decision I ever made. Economists will tell you that every boom is followed by a bust, as sure as every sunrise is followed by a sunset. And it's always darkest right after they cut off your electricity.

One year after that initial phone call, the United States faced a financial crisis, and the entire mortgage industry was on the brink of collapse, and collapse it did, in spectacular fashion, and took the world economy down with it. If you haven't seen the movie *The Big Short*, I suggest you give it a watch. It's one thing to know that toxic mortgage "backed" securities changed life on this planet as we know it; it's another thing to hear the story of how that happened, because stories are more powerful than spread sheets.

Not only did my friend lose his job, he also lost his only source of income. He truly believed that his one source of income would be consistent forever and that he had security in his position. But, unfortunately, my friend was now out of work with no way to pay his bills.

After losing his job, he would tell me: "I was only as good as my last sale."

Instead of closing my business to pursue the lure of a single paycheck, I decided to dedicate myself to growing my business and finding ways to stabilize my income through recurring revenue streams. I would deal with the hardships of hiring employees and working tirelessly to make money, but this time, I would focus on building a business that lasts. I would not be defined by a single paycheck or my last sale, but by the value of my business.

Eventually, I would build my own money-making machine that allowed me to experience financial freedom. When I eventually sold my business, I knew I made the right decision. In the following chapters I will teach you how to be in a position to make a similar decision.

Selling A Business Is Not Easy

Surprising statistic, 20 percent of all small businesses fail in their first year, 30 percent fail in their second year, and 50 percent fail after five years in business. Finally, 70 percent of all small businesses that do survive fail in their tenth year of business.[1] (Small businesses are defined as businesses with fewer than 500 employees). How is this

---

[1] Georgia McIntyre. "What Percentage of Small Businesses Fail? (And Other Need-to-Know Stats)" Fundera.com, June 21, 2019. https://www.fundera.com/blog/what-percentage-of-small-businesses-fail. Article shares statistics from the U.S. Bureau of Labor Statistics Business Employment Dynamics report found here: https://www.bls.gov/bdm/us_age_naics_00_table7.txt. Accessed August 29, 2019.

possible? According to a U.S. Bank study, 82 percent of businesses that fail do so because of cash flow problems. In order to survive, you need to get the money right, and getting the money right requires designing a business model with consistent income that can survive without you.

Although many business owners have a dream of growing their business into a money machine and selling it one day, most will fail. They fail because the owner hires his no-good brother-in-law, to keep his wife happy. Oh, if it were only that simple. *They fail because they do not have a picture in their mind of what a money machine looks like.* That is unfortunate, because most business owners who do make money make the majority of their money when they sell.

Consider this: If farmers can see the harvest in their minds before they plant the first seed, why can't business owners see their future business model?

The reason is that business owners get caught up in the day-to-day operation of the business. They are focused on daily sales or employee attitudes or the latest technologies. They fail to strategize and focus on the big picture of the business. They fail to learn from the past, live in the present, and plan for the end.

By not starting with the end in mind, most small business owners fail to turn their businesses into money-making machines. As author Michael Gerber said in his classic book, *The E-Myth*, they continue to work *in their business* and not *on their business.*[2] The tragic truth is they do not know how to create a consistent money-making machine that gives them financial freedom.

---

[2] Michael E. Gerber. *The E-Myth: Why Most Small Businesses Don't Work and What to Do about It* (New York: HarperBusiness, 2001).

Financial Freedom: Having steady cash flow from your business, and the time to enjoy it.

Small business owners understand how to do the work, but often fail to understand the business itself. Business owners operate according to what the owner wants, which is usually a place to work freely, and they fail to understand what the business truly needs, which is independence, growth and consistency. And as Gerber tells us, "If your business depends on you, you don't own a business; you own a job."

Business owners start a business because they believe that they can do the job better than another employer. They feel that they can provide a better service or product to a customer. They feel that if you want something done right, you do it yourself. These people, who believe they can make a difference in the world, will wake up one day, quit their jobs, and decide to set out on their own. In short, most will sober up, leave their jobs and pursue their dreams of starting a business. They are the ones for whom I wrote this book. To paraphrase Freddie Mercury, "They are the champions, my friend, and they will keep on thinking about the end." We are the champions, my friends. Learn from the past, live in the present, and focus on the end.

The employee-turned-business owner believes that starting a business will allow him or her the freedom to run a business that is not limited to a paycheck. "No more will someone tell me how much money I can or can't make." There is a problem, however, with this mindset. The problem is that the mindset of an employee is completely different from a small-business-owner mindset. A business owner needs to see the future of the business, unlike an employee, who only needs to focus on the task at hand, until quitting time.

Truly talented business owners like George W. Murphy of Hawaii (the main character in this book) can see the future of their businesses, and this is why they are successful. These entrepreneurs can paint the big picture in their minds from the very start of the business.

The number of business owners who cannot sell their businesses is enormous. According to various expert estimates, 70 to 85 percent of all business owners cannot sell their businesses. According to an article in *The New York Times*, you can see this by reviewing the number of businesses listed for sale each month on BizBuySell. com, which facilitates business sales. Less than 5 percent of all companies listed on the site will be sold successfully. This means many business owners who dedicated their lives to their businesses will fail to find buyers.

The small business owner is the sole reason a company exists, as well as the biggest reason why most owners will never realize the power and financial freedom that comes with owning a business. If the owner leaves, there will be no business.

It's especially hard to sell a consulting or advisory business. The *Times* article observes, "Clients come to depend on their advisers for help. When advisers leave the business, their clients often go with them. In reality, the clients are not the customers of the business; they are customers of the advisors."[3] Although it may be hard to sell a consulting business, there are ways to implement recurring revenue to stabilize your income and create a business that is sellable. Smart spouses insist on a prenuptial agreement, even if they have no intention of splitting. Smart business owners plan for divorce, as the marriage will take care of itself. Love is blind, but divorce is 20/20.

---

[3] Josh Patrick. "Why Many Small Businesses Cannot Be Sold," You're The Boss blog, *The New York Times*, September 4, 2014. https://boss.blogs.nytimes.com/2014/09/04/why-many-small-businesses-cannot-be-sold/. Accessed August 29, 2019.

Smart business owners believe that you should grow a business that can be sold, even if you have no intention of selling. The best businesses in the world are salable.

Having a clear vision of where you are and where you want to go will give you clarity on how you run your business and ultimately how you live your life. Either way, all business owners will need to know the right way to grow a business and the right way to plan their exit. Again, getting into business, like getting into a marriage, is easy. Getting out of a business, like getting out of a marriage, with all of your assets, can be the hard part.

You don't have to be psychic to see the future of your business (although it wouldn't hurt); you just need to know what to focus on.

The good news is that, for many businesses, it's surprisingly easy to create what I call an Aloha Money Machine if you know what to look for and what to focus on. What is an Aloha Money Machine? The next chapter explains this powerful idea.

2

The Solution: Create Your Aloha Money Machine

y fascination with being rich in business started when I was a little kid, hearing stories of a man who started from nothing, built a business, and became one of the richest self-made men in Hawaii.

As a child, I heard stories of how this man owned the largest General Motors (GM) dealership in the world (Aloha Motors, a dealership that sat where the $200-million-dollar Honolulu Convention center sits today) and how he owned several businesses and made millions on a single deal. This man was a giant in the business world and a legend in Hawaii. This man also just so happened to be my grandfather.

"Rich Grandfather," as I referred to him, was actually my great-grandfather on my dad's side. I refer to him as my Rich Grandfather, as my grandfather on my mom's side was a house painter and not considered rich. Rich Granddad, Poor Granddad, could have been the title of this book, but I didn't want to sit around waiting for the cease and desist letter from Robert Kiyosaki.

Rich Grandfather would learn the secrets to his business formula, which I nicknamed the Aloha Money Machine as a business owner. These are the same secrets I used to build my own business.

Hawaii Convention Center

Not only did Rich Grandfather open several car dealerships around the world that all produced a steady flow of recurring revenue, but he also used the same system in several different businesses other than selling autos. These included a taxi business, a construction business, a manufacturing business, a tool business, an oil business, and a real estate business, to name just a few.

Something More Valuable Than Money

Although he started poor, went bankrupt twice and lost everything, George Murphy was able to replicate the business system over and over again with triumphant results.

Rich Grandfather had something more valuable than money: He had the knowledge of how to turn a normal business into an extraordinary business; in other words, businesses that were money-making machines.

Napoleon Hill, an OG in the self-help industry, once interviewed quite a number of the most successful people in the world. He asked all of them the same questions about what constituted their riches. After interviewing 500 people, Hill came up with a list of twelve riches of life. Surprisingly, out of the list of twelve, only one answer had anything to do with money. That answer that was consistent among the rich interviewees was a need for economic security through the knowledge of how to make money. Wealth-destroying events like government intervention, divorce, economic crashes, betting against the Patriots in the Superbowl or misfortune can happen to anyone, but the knowledge of how to create a money-making machine lives on forever.

Although Rich Grandfather went bankrupt two different times, he knew how to make money through a system. Because this system was repeatable, he was able to earn back his fortune several times.

Rich Grandfather's Rags-to-Riches-to-Rags-to-Riches-to-Rags Story

It's easy to understand how to make money by working. You interview at a restaurant, get hired at that restaurant, you start washing dishes, and eventually, you get paid for the work that was done. The concept of working to make money is easy to understand, but what is difficult to understand is the concept of building a money machine that continuously pumps out money regardless of how many dishes you wash.

An incredible thing about Rich Grandfather is not only the system that he designed, but that he was an average man with a seventh grade education who started from nothing. He was poor, grew up on a farm, and became incredibly rich in business by his own willpower. I was fascinated that a man with the same blood as me could achieve so much in his life in such a short time. But as great as he was, he was also a mystery. As a young man I still didn't know how he did it. How did he create his money-making machine? And how did he lose all of his money shortly after he died? They say "You can't take it with you," but it turns out, when you die, they can take it away from you.

Build Your Aloha Money Machine

The solution for not failing in business is to follow Rich Grandfather's formula and build your own Aloha Money Machine.

It's fitting to call the formula the Aloha Money Machine, being that my grandfather built his own money machine called Aloha Motors, and that I was born and raised in Hawaii.

In fact, I was born on Rich Grandfather's ranch in 1977, twelve years after he was named Hawaii's Businessman of the Year (there was no Businesswoman of the year, as it was 1965) on the island of Molokai. Pu'u O Hoku Ranch on Molokai is a 14,000-acre ranch that takes up almost the entire eastern end of the island. It was an exciting time for my parents and a great place to be born.

My dad was a cowboy (*paniolo*) who grew a popular cash crop, weed (*pakalolo*) in the mountains and surfed every time the waves were up. It was a good life for my dad. But for my mom, living on the ranch on Molokai was too slow. So, when I was three, my parents moved to the mainland, where I would live until I was eight years old.

At eight years old, I would move back to Hawaii, but this time it would be to the Big Island, not the island of Molokai. On the big island I would attend Kealakehe Elementary and graduate from Konawaena High School.

Despite my family's long history in Hawaii, the meaning of *aloha* in the Aloha Money Machine is much deeper than being born and raised in Hawaii. In Hawaii, the word *aloha* means hello and goodbye. It's used when you first meet someone and is used when you say farewell to a close friend. In business, the most important words you can say are "Not guilty, Your Honor." Actually, the two most important words are *hello* and *goodbye*. The starting and ending dates in business are the most significant dates for all business owners. Rich Grandfather was successful because he planned from the start what he wanted his business to look like at the end. He learned from the past, lived in the present, and focused on the end.

The goal behind the Aloha Money Machine is to build a consistent machine that can thrive regardless of the owner's involvement. The formula outlined in the book is intended to help business owners develop their own Aloha Money Machine that continuously produces cash on a regular basis.

Although *aloha* means hello and goodbye, it's important to note that the word *aloha* also has a secret meaning. *Aloha* means much more than any definition you will find in a dictionary. In Hawaii, you hear *aloha* all the time. You hear people say, "Have aloha," "Be aloha," and, "No aloha." *Aloha* is so much more than hello and goodbye. *Aloha,* by its true definition, is a way of life and the real power behind the Aloha Money Machine.

Once you create your own Aloha Money Machine that spits out cash on a regular basis, you will have successfully created an asset. Having an asset will give you options, and options can give you wealth. To paraphrase John Warrillow in his book *Built to Sell*, growing your business into an asset might be the best shot most of us will have at a comfortable retirement. Once you create an asset, you may want to expand the business, sell the business, or hold on to the business, feeling confident knowing that you could sell your business anytime, if you needed to. Remember, no matter what you do with the business, you should build it to be sold, even if you have no intention of ever selling.

In the last chapter of this book, I will give you examples of how to build a business that changes the world. I will also give you some examples of how to avoid the mistakes Rich Grandfather made and how to live a life of meaning. That's probably more than you bargained for and a lot to ask of a book of this length, but it was easy. Why? Well, as you might imagine, I began this book with how I wanted it to end in mind.

Additionally, I will show you examples of how the biggest companies in the world, like Uber and Airbnb, are changing the world using the Aloha Money Machine philosophy. These example companies and similar companies of the past have all resembled a similar business model to become successful. You can, too.

Using the Aloha Money Machine system to start businesses will not only generate consistent cash but will also give you the freedom to possibly help others as well. This philosophy of Aloha Money Machine is summed up as: "Help others become rich, so you can become rich yourself." Or, as the great Zig Ziglar famously said, "You will get all you want in life, if you help enough other people get what they want." This is the true secret behind the Aloha Money Machine success.

My Aloha Money Machine Story

As a little boy, I remember sitting on the living room floor of my dad's beaten-up apartment, staring at a single blow-up mattress in the middle of the room, hearing stories of Rich Grandfather's success and how he had so much. I was captivated by the story but also remember thinking, "How is it possible that my grandfather had so much, and we have so little?" How was it possible that here we were, sitting in an empty room with no furniture or refrigerator, and only a few years prior, Rich Grandfather had a Learjet and a fleet of airplanes at his disposal.

When I was born, Rich Grandfather was a very old man living a quiet life in his penthouse in Honolulu. At that time of his life, his health was failing, and the remaining businesses that he owned had either been sold or were held in the trust of his attorneys. The once-mighty and bold businessman of Hawaii was now an old, weak man, unable to manage his businesses. The money that he did receive from the sale of businesses he used for medical and living expenses with nothing to spare.

When I was a young boy, I loved the stories of my Rich Grandfather's accomplishments. But I wanted to know how he had done it. How had he built his businesses and how did he become so rich? I was so curious about his success that I would ask my dad to repeat stories of the great Rich Grandfather to uncover hidden clues left behind. Hey, you can keep your Werther's Orginal hard candies, what I wanted from my Rich Grandfather was hidden clues as to how to make and keep money.

I often asked to visit Rich Grandfather, but every time I asked, the answer was always the same. "Why do you want to see him? He's probably too busy for us." Or, "If he wanted to see us, he would call us," Dad said. It was no secret—there was an underlying resistance to seeing or even talking to Rich Grandfather, but I always thought it was because he was intimidating, and his success threatened people.

It seemed possible in my young mind that Rich Grandfather would call my dad out for living in a crappy apartment, living paycheck-to-paycheck, or not having a refrigerator. I imagined Rich Grandfather would say something like, "What are you doing with your life?

When I was thirty years old, I had already bought and sold fifteen businesses and was a multimillionaire. At your age in my thirties, I had enough cash that I almost bought Coca-Cola, Studebaker, and Hawaiian Airlines!"

No one wants to hear someone say he was a multimillionaire at your age when you're currently living in a shitty apartment, so I never questioned my dad's hesitation to see Rich Grandfather. But I was always so curious about how my Rich Grandfather made all his money through business. At five years old, living on the mainland, I made the decision that I would never live in a shitty apartment again, and that I would follow in the footsteps of my Rich Grandfather to be successful. I began with the end in mind, to be successful. I would learn from the past (my rich Grandfather's successes), live in the present and focus on the end. Not bad for a five year old! I guess I truly am my Rich Grandfather's grandson.

At age five, all I had were the stories of my Rich Grandfather's accomplishments left behind in the wake of this greatness. What did I know? I knew that I wanted to be successful. I knew that I wanted to have money. I knew that I wanted people to respect me, and I knew that I wanted to be remembered for all the incredible things I had achieved in life. But I honestly didn't know what business success looked like firsthand, so I made it my goal to uncover the truth to Rich Grandfather's fortune and fame.

In his time, Rich Grandfather was featured in magazines, billboards, commercials, radio, and news articles. He played as if there were no rules. He was the first in the office and the last one to leave. He was a hard drinker who could handle his alcohol, and he was a maverick of his time. He was loved for what he was able to accomplish and achieve. As a boy, I looked up to this man and wanted to be like him.

I wanted to achieve my own goal of being rich, and in some strange way, I wanted him to be proud of me. Most of all I wanted to get rid of that air mattress and buy a refrigerator.

Details and personal stories that I learned about the mystery of Rich Grandfather stuck with me and shaped me into the man I am today. He was my inspiration for building businesses and having a goal to be a millionaire. Because of him and the life lessons I learned, I achieved my goal of being rich and became a millionaire at thirty-one years old. And the first thing I did was buy my dad a refrigerator.

The Start Of A Big Chicken

My parents divorced when I was four years old, shortly after moving to the mainland. Although I never saw my mom and dad fight, I do remember hard feelings and very emotional times. To make it worse, I was also having a hard time in school and falling behind academically from the rest of my classmates. I would find out the reason I was struggling in school was that I had a learning disability. I was later diagnosed with dyslexia. What I did not know at the time, that I do know now, is that dyslexia is in fact my superpower, at least according to an article about dyslexia and entrepreneurs in *The New York Times*:

> *It has long been known that dyslexics are drawn to running their own businesses, where they can get around their weaknesses in reading and writing and play to their strengths. But a new study of entrepreneurs in the United States suggests that dyslexia is much more common among small-business owners than even the experts had thought.*

The report, compiled by Julie Logan, a professor of entrepreneurship at the Cass Business School in London, found that more than a third of the entrepreneurs she surveyed—35 percent—identified themselves as dyslexic. The study also concluded that dyslexics were more likely than nondyslexics to delegate authority and to excel in oral communication and problem solving and were twice as likely to own two or more businesses.

"We found that dyslexics who succeed had overcome an awful lot in their lives by developing compensatory skills," Logan said during an interview. "If you tell your friends and acquaintances that you plan to start a business, you'll hear over and over, 'It won't work. It can't be done.' But dyslexics are extraordinarily creative about maneuvering their way around problems." [4]

Although these were tough times, I was still proud to have been born in Hawaii. Friends on the mainland would ask me about Hawaii and how awesome it must have been living there. Being born in Hawaii and having a long family history in the state made me feel unique and special. It also helped that I had a unique Hawaiian middle name. At school, people would ask me, "Is your middle name Hawaiian? How do you say it?" *Moanui* is pronounced *mo-ah-NEW-ee*, I would say. Teachers would ask, "What does it mean?"

"I was named after a stream on the Island of Molokai where I was born," I would say. The stream was, in fact, a beautiful stream that flowed from the lush green mountains where waterfalls were frequently seen. Water gathers in the mountains and gently flows

---

[4] Brent Bowers. "Study shows stronger links between entrepreneurs and dyslexia," *The New York Times*, November 5, 2007. https://www.nytimes.com/2007/12/05/business/worldbusiness/05iht-dyslexia.4.8602036.html. Accessed August 21, 2019.

into a beautiful ocean bay that faces the Island of Maui. My parents were living the natural, hippie lifestyle where my mom made all of our clothes and dad had a garden of the aforementioned, now almost legal in Hawaii, cash crop *pakalolo* (marijuana). They picked my name, as it was a beautiful place. But unfortunately, my parents failed to pay attention to the meaning. They figured that some names don't have meaning, but they were wrong.

As time went on, my frustrations with school started to increase. I now believed the lie: I was stupid, and I would never be a success. I became extremely shy and very angry. I feared that people would look at me differently. They would think of me as stupid. I would be humiliated in public. Seeing this anger and my downward spiral, my parents decided that I would move to Kailua-Kona, on the Big Island of Hawaii with my dad as we had family on the island.

At eight years old, I moved back to Hawaii and made friends quickly. Life was good at the time until the day I found out the true meaning of my middle name. For years I had been proud of my name, as it connected me to a place that I loved, but this would change quickly.

One day on my way to school a friend who was born and raised on the Big Island asked me, "Brah, what's your middle name?"

"Moanui," I said.

"Braddah, you know your middle name means *big chicken*, right? You one big chicken," he said, smiling.

"Big chicken?" I asked.

"Yep. Huge chicken," he replied.

There was no escape. I was caught. They'd figured me out. I was a fraud. I thought that I could move to Hawaii and hide my identity, but I was wrong. I thought that if I hid my identity that no one would think that I was stupid and I could have a normal life. Before I could run and hide, however, everyone in my neighborhood knew my name was *big chicken*.

As time went on and the teasing slowed down, I continued to hide my learning disability. But in the back of my mind, I still considered my self a huge chicken. I was chicken for hiding that I had a learning disability, and I was chicken to hide the fact that I had big dreams of one day starting my own business and becoming successful. I was a big chicken because thanks to my middle name, when it came to succeeding in life and business, I was plucked.

In high school, as a senior, I struggled to find my path (it could have been from enjoying some of my dad's cash crop, but more likely it was due to my dyslexia). I didn't know what I would do once I graduated, so I decided to talk to a high school counselor for direction. He said that the school had just received a brand-new machine for students just like me who didn't know what to do or be after high school.

"With this computer (the size of a minivan), you simply enter your interests, personal behaviors, and learning styles, and the device will calculate the very best profession for you," he said.

I logged onto the computer, answered the questions, and the computer processed my life's career. It took some time to come up with the answer, but when it finally did, it said that the best fit for me, a big chicken, would be working at a KFC, where else? What better place for a big chicken. Actually, the computer said I was well suited to be a bus driver. I didn't want to drive a bus. Pluck that.

In 1995, I would graduate from Konawaena High School on the Big Island of Hawaii. I would follow the recommendation of my parents and continue my traditional schooling in college, as I didn't want to be a bus driver. I flew from the Island of Hawaii to the desert of Reno, Nevada, to attend my first year of college at Truckee Meadows Community College.

After a year in Reno, I decided that the desert was not for me, so I hopped into my old gray Nissan truck and drove to Santa Barbara. I would spend the next three years in Santa Barbara, where I attended community college part-time and drank beer full time. Well, everybody in college has to major in something and I chose Liquid Studies. Yes, I was well on my way to an AA degree, not an Associate of Arts degree, but a "Hi, I'm Big Chicken, and I'm an alcoholic" degree.

But luckily, after three years, I found myself moving once again to slow down my drinking and continue my college education. This time I moved to San Diego, where I would attend San Diego State University for one year. Although I loved the independence of college, I was still struggling to find my path in life. If you don't know where you want your story to end it's difficult to find the beginning. You need to know, "Once upon a time…what happened."

I was having a hard time, and I didn't know what I would do once I graduated from college, so once again, I decided to talk to a guidance counselor for direction. The counselor said, "The school just installed a new program for students like you. With this computer (smaller than the first one, but still the size of a Mini Cooper), you merely enter your interests, personal behaviors, and learning styles. Then the computer will calculate the very best profession for you." Yeah right, I'd ridden that bus before.

I logged into the computer, answered the questions, and the computer calculated my life's career. This time it didn't say bus driver. It said office administrator. I'm not sure that was an improvement. Although, at least on the bus, I'd be in charge.

From an early age, I always wanted to be great. I always wanted to succeed, I always wanted to be rich, and I knew that driving a bus or answering the telephone at someone else's business would not get me to the place I wanted to go. Feeling confused and depressed, I flew back to the Big Island of Hawaii, where my dad lived, to regroup. There were mornings when it was all I could do to crawl off the air mattress, paste on a smile and move through my day like I knew where my life was headed.

I will never forget the conversation I had with my father. It was a beautiful day in Hawaii when my dad picked me up at the airport in his beaten-up 1991 white Toyota truck. As we drove down the street, he obviously saw my frustration and the difficulty I was having. He told me a story that proved to be useful in my own life. This was the story of his high school gym teacher.

Dad described him as a slow old man in his seventies who would always talk about retiring, but who had made some bad financial choices as a younger man. There he was, still teaching at seventy years old at some crappy high school. He was an angry and bitter man. The first day of school, he walked into the gym, looked at the students, and said if anyone wanted to get an A in the class, he or she would have to beat him at racquetball.

He would teach the students the basics of racquetball but expected everyone to train on their own. At the end of the semester, they would have to all play against him to receive their final grade.

My dad recalled that he wanted to beat this old man so badly that he would train every day. "Yes, I wanted to beat him to receive an A for the class, but most of all, I wanted to teach this bitter old man a lesson," said Dad.

At the end of the semester, my dad was the best in his class at racquetball, and was easily beating his other classmates. In high school, my dad was exceptionally strong. Dad would hit the ball so hard that most of his classmates didn't even have time to react. After beating his fellow classmates, he was feeling confident, and it was now time to play his teacher for the final grade.

Dad walked into the gymnasium, took off his shirt, flexed his muscles, and bounced around the room in preparation for meeting his opponent. A few moments later his teacher slowly opened the door. They both looked each other in the eye, and the teacher said, "Let's play."

This day his teacher seemed surprisingly tired and showed no emotion on his face.

My dad served the ball with all his strength. The old man responded by hitting the ball perfectly into the corner of the wall, where the ball dropped to the ground out of reach of my father's racket. My dad served again with all of his might, and the old man responded with a perfect hit once again. This happened again and again until the final score was 0 to 15. My dad had not only lost; he hadn't scored a single point.

In frustration, my dad demanded a rematch. The teacher agreed, and my dad played even harder. By the end of the game, sweat was pouring down my dad's face, and he was bleeding on his elbows from continuously running into the wall.

At the end of the rematch game, the score was 5 to 15 with the old man winning again. Before the old man walked out of the room to call in his next opponent, he turned to my dad and said, "All you get is a C."

My dad was furious and said to the old man, "I'm quicker and stronger than you. How is it possible for you to beat me?"

The old man turned back around and said, "It's not strength or quickness that wins games, but the placement of the ball that wins games. You need to know where the ball is going before you ever set foot on the court. You need to envision where you want the ball to go before you ever hit the ball. If you can see where you want the ball to go, you will win every time."

My dad shared this story with me as an example to teach me to keep my eye on the prize. What did I want out of life, and what did I want my life to look like at its end?

"God rewards those with specific goals," Dad said.

I took my dad's story to heart. Rich Grandfather also believed if you genuinely value your goals, you must reject things that don't propel you to achieve your goal. I knew that I didn't want to work for someone else and that I didn't need a college degree to open my own business. I also knew that if I wanted to be rich, I would need to build a business just like Rich Grandfather. My actions needed to reflect on my goals, so when I returned to San Diego, I dropped out of San Diego State University to start my own business. Some of the most successful people on the planet are college dropouts, including Bill Gates, who, most everyone would agree, has created one of the largest and most profitable Money Machines of all time. I'm editing this book using one of Microsoft's programs.

My Start In The Furniture Delivery Business

Although I was fearful of the future, I dropped out of college to start a business of my own. At the time, my mother and stepdad owned a little furniture store in Encinitas, California. I did furniture deliveries from time to time to make money, but I didn't officially have a business. I still owned my Nissan truck from Reno, and I was eager to make money. I was also strong, so naturally, carrying heavy objects was the easiest way to make money.

I started a one-person furniture delivery business while I researched how Rich Grandfather had built his fortune. I didn't yet know the formula and I couldn't ask Rich Grandfater, short of having a séance, as he had passed away ten years earlier. I did know that he had built businesses and sold them for a profit. That was what I was going to do, as well. I would drive my little truck around the city, hand out business cards, and advertise my furniture delivery service. The business cards read, "Murf's Reliable Furniture Delivery." My goal was to build the business and eventually sell it.

I was so hungry to grow my own business that I would take any delivery job that was offered to me. I delivered pianos. I delivered building equipment to construction sites. I delivered bad news. I even delivered people to the airport. I was willing to deliver anyone or anything for the right price. I would have delivered a baby, if someone had called and asked. But the bread-and-butter of the business was always furniture deliveries. If my phone rang for furniture deliveries, I would drop everything to accommodate that delivery. I never missed an appointment and because of this I had enough business income to pay for my living expenses, which ultimately justified my decision to finally tell my parents that I dropped out of college. Hey, dropping out is easy; telling the parents that you have is far more difficult.

My dad used to tell me that Rich Grandfather would only sleep a few hours at most; then he was back to work. I once read in a 1967 interview that Rich Grandfather was so stimulated by growing his business. "I can't do anything else. I've worked twenty hours a day, seven days a week, for the past thirty years," he said.[5]

I originally believed the secret to growing a business was to do everything myself and work tirelessly until the job was done. But to my disappointment, I couldn't achieve business success working seven days a week. In the beginning, I would wake up at 5:00 a.m. to plan the day by organizing my schedule, printing invoices and locating delivery addresses using a thick bound book of street maps before the advent of smartphones and GPS. Anybody remember the Thomas Brothers Guide? Who were the Thomas Brothers and why were they so into maps? Do you think Google Maps drove them out of business? Or maybe they learned from the past, lived in the present, focused on the end and saw the GPS coming and sold their Money Machine, before it was too late. I hope so.

I would meet my first customer at 7:00 a.m., working from 7:00 a.m. to 7:00 p.m. six days a week delivering furniture. Most days, I would get home at 8:00 p.m., then spend the next hour calling back customers to schedule appointments for the following day. The last hour was spent entering customer information into my customer management software. I consistently kept a log of all the activities and deliveries that I had done on a daily basis, as I knew this detailed information would eventually help me build my business. I then used my database to call past clients for any additional delivery needs they might have. I officially ended the day at 11:00 p.m., ate dinner, went to bed, and did it all again the next day. Lather, rinse, repeat. Hey, it works for Head & Shoulders, but it was not working for me.

I worked like a madman because I knew Rich Grandfather had done the same thing. I was willing to sacrifice everything to accomplish

---

[5] Dale Johnson, "GM's Biggest Dealer - From Saskatchewan," *Regina Leader-Post*, July 24, 2008.

my goal; I sacrificed friendships, relationships, I sacrificed chickens (kidding, I'm a vegetarian) and even time with family, as I was ready to do whatever it took to grow my business. But the problem was that I was getting burned out. I was burning the candle at both ends and dynamiting it in the middle.

Starting A Refinishing Business

As my sales grew, so did my income. Although I was tempted to buy a new car and spend money on luxuries, I was also disciplined. I knew that the only way to grow my business was to save money. I did this by setting up an automatic bank transfer every month. Every month, 10 percent of my total gross income would be transferred to a savings account, which I would later use to grow my business.

At the age of twenty-one, I was making $100,000 a year and growing the business quickly. But I knew that if I wanted to be rich I couldn't do everything myself. Even at twenty-one years old, I already knew that personally moving furniture was only a temporary job. The act of carrying heavy furniture on a regular basis was taking a toll on my back and physical health. In my business I was literally doing the heavy lifting.

I also noticed that if I didn't work, I didn't get paid. What if I got hurt and couldn't work? If I couldn't work, my business would fail, and I needed to find a way to protect myself from this. I didn't see how it would be possible to become rich from a business making an hourly wage. Even if I made $1,000.00 an hour, I would still have to work every hour. Rich Grandfather didn't work every hour to build his empire. How could he? He was an old man. It's physically impossible to make as much as he did by working an hourly wage. I knew if I wanted to be rich, I would have to find a way to make money regardless of whether I worked or not.

Although I knew that I needed to hire employees and buy a real moving truck, I was still hesitant to do so. I knew that retaining employees would protect me if I got hurt and was unable to work, but I was hesitant, as I felt good and I was in good shape. I also knew that if I hired employees, I would make less money per delivery because I would have to pay for their salary. I knew as well that once I employed a full-time employee, I would lose some control of the business. I didn't want to lose control of the business; I liked the way I ran it. Why did I need to hire someone to do my job when I was the best employee the company had? But I knew that Rich Grandfather had employees and that he developed businesses that ran regardless of his physical involvement and I needed to copy that system.

Although I would make less money per delivery and would lose some control of the business, I decided to hire full-time employees. I knew that I needed to switch my focus from doing the physical work to growing the business. Not too long after my decision to grow the business, a new opportunity would show itself.

Every business owner will face "opportunity costs" in one way or another. He or she can decide to keep the business model the same, or change the business model to take advantage of the new opportunity. Choosing to do something means you also make a choice not to do something, that's the definition of opportunity cost. Analyzing opportunity costs helps business owners determine the highest and best use of their time. And that is exactly what I did.

It was a typical sunny day in San Diego delivering furniture, but this day was a little different. I was delivering outdoor teak patio furniture, not the traditional dining room furniture. Teak is a precious wood known for its durability and tolerance to insects. The customer to whom I was delivering patio furniture was a very rich homeowner in the upscale Rancho Santa Fe community. The home was a beautiful, single-story, modern design with lush tropical landscaping surrounding it. When I arrived, the homeowner, a woman in her thirties, greeted me in the middle of the large circular driveway. She told me to carry the new patio furniture to the back of the house and place the furniture next to the waterfall by the Olympic-sized pool.

As soon as I delivered the new furniture in the location she wanted, she shrieked with disgust. "This is horrible!" the woman said. She looked at the new furniture; then she turned and looked at some old gray patio furniture sitting next to it. The homeowner had bought a few pieces of patio furniture a few weeks prior, and the wood was already gray and weathered. (It is common for untreated wood furniture to turn gray with exposure to the ultraviolet rays of the sun.)

She shook her head slowly and compared the old gray furniture to the new furniture and said, "What am I going to do with this? This will not work!" Then she turned to me and asked if I had ever done furniture refinishing before. She wanted to know if I could refinish her old, gray furniture and make it look new like the new furniture I was delivering.

Being the entrepreneur that I am and seeing a new way to make money, I quickly said yes. I had never refinished furniture before, but I would give it a try—how hard could it be? I finished the delivery job and scheduled a time to come back and do the refinishing work. The task was to refinish four gray chairs and one table to make it look new again. The plan was to complete all the work in a day, so I based the cost of the job to the equivalent of one day's pay for deliveries. I gave the homeowner the bill, and she happily agreed on the price, but the job turned out to be a lot more work than I originally expected.

The one-day job turned out to be three full days of work. It was awful work as well. It was backbreaking, on-my-hands-and-knees work. To refinish the patio furniture required sanding between every crack and crevices of the slatted wood. To make matters worse, the sanding had to be done by hand, as the electric palm sanders could not fit between the slats. I spent the next three days sanding furniture until my hands were bleeding and aching with pain. The materials that I used were also horrible. They were hard to use, messy, and very expensive.

I finished the job only to lose money. The cost of materials alone didn't even cover my quoted price. Walking away from the job, I told myself that I would never do that kind of work again. However, as luck would have it, the very next day I was faced with the same fate. Once again, I was delivering teak patio furniture, and once again, the homeowner was asking me to refinish existing furniture. I thought to myself that I would never do furniture refinishing again, but then I remembered Rich Grandfather. What would my Rich Grandfather say? He would say, "Never turn down an opportunity to make money, boy!"

I decided it would be best to give this new homeowner a price out of courtesy. I would give her a price to show her I wanted to help, but sorry, I simply couldn't. I quoted her a price so enormous it equaled the same amount I would have earned delivering furniture for one whole week. I remember giving her the quote thinking that no one in his or her right mind would pay the price. And to my surprise, without hesitation, she agreed to the price. I was utterly shocked that someone would spend that kind of money on refinishing furniture! Either she wasn't in her right mind, or I was in the wrong business. Had I not chosen that enormous amount, I would have literally left money on the table.

I must have been staring at her for some time as she interrupted my awkwardness and said, "How about I give you $200 more to make it worth your time?" I knew from that moment I was on to a new business opportunity.

Later that night, I analyzed my opportunity costs. I researched my competition, calculated my expenses if I bought supplies in bulk, and determined that I would make more money refinishing furniture than making deliveries. Within a few days, I had changed my whole business from "Murf's Reliable Furniture Delivery" to "Expert Furniture Refinishing." I changed the name of my company and started refinishing furniture full-time. Was I an expert in furniture refinishing? No. But hey, this is a business plan, not a documentary, and besides, I soon would be.

I knew with the low competition and the demand from affluent homeowners willing to pay top dollar for this service, I could quickly grow the business and eventually develop a system for recurring revenue. My next goal would be to build a system and hire employees to follow the path of Rich Grandfather.

Because of the experience running my own furniture delivery business, I knew that I needed separate systems for the different parts of the business. I developed a system for invoicing, customer service, marketing, scheduling appointments, purchasing, and refinishing. With my systems in place, I hired my first employee. My first employee would be an office assistant. I would have her follow my written system, and I kept track of her daily activities. As time went on, we would periodically update the system to increase productivity. This freed up my time and helped me focus on completing the refinishing jobs in one day.

The second employee I hired was a part-time bookkeeper who helped me keep track of the financials and the health of my business. Although both employees were amazing, the day I hired my first full-time labor technician was an incredible day. No longer would I be the only one to physically sand every piece of furniture by hand. I was now able to accomplish more jobs in a day, and in return, this allowed me the freedom to finally think like a business owner. No longer would I have to think like an employee and do all the work myself; now I could take the time to studiously grow my business. Although I was a really good hand-sander of furniture, I would soon find out that the best use of my time was talking to my customers. I now had more time to focus on my customers, who ultimately wrote the checks that grew my business.

As time went on, I positioned myself as a passive owner. It was not essential that I was involved in the day-to-day operation of the business. I developed a system that my employees followed and a system for managing the system. Because I had a method for managing the system, I could work at the office or from a remote location of my choosing. I had a system for inventory, invoicing, and collecting payment. I developed a marketing system for generating new and repeat business. I also developed a mobile refinishing system for completing jobs at my customers' homes.

Before this time, no one was doing mobile refinishing. Furniture refinishing companies were known to drive to the customers' homes, pick up the furniture, then drive back to their warehouses to do the work. Once my competition was back at their warehouse, they would set up a time to do the work, then schedule a time to deliver the furniture back to the customer's home after the work was completed. This time-consuming process took five to seven days.

My mobile system allowed us to complete jobs in one day or less. This system streamlined the business, saving time, allowing us to cut operating expenses by 50 percent, and ultimately allowed me to make more money.

The system also allowed me as the business owner to take a big-picture approach to business. Because I no longer had to do each job myself, I could now focus my attention on what made me the most money. I would find out that if I focused my attention on commercial establishments (resorts, hotels, or shopping centers), I would make a lot more money.

Instead of refinishing two or three pieces of furniture, we could refinish 200 or 300 pieces of furniture at one time. I also focused my attention on establishing a repeat maintenance program for all my past and present customers. I knew that if I could establish maintenance contracts with these people and companies, I could create a recurring revenue stream that would increase the value of the business.

Creating a maintenance program gave me the recurring revenue I had always dreamed of. The recurring revenue turned out to be a good portion of my company's income, which remained for the life of my business. I would find that this consistent cash flow turned my small business into a valuable asset overnight. (Recurring revenue is the portion of a company's revenue that is expected to continue in the future. Unlike one-off sales, these revenues are predictable, stable and can be counted on to occur at regular intervals going forward with a relatively high degree of certainty.)[6]

Although I had my share of problems with employees who were snorting meth on the job to keep their spirits up and defecating in

---

[6] Investopedia.com, Recurring Revenue page. https://www.investopedia.com/terms/r/recurringrevenue. asp. Accessed August 21, 2019.

the back of my work trucks, my business stayed steady. The company consistently generated a stream of cash every month for more than ten years. Knowing what I wanted from the start of my business, and following my Rich Grandfather's philosophy of building a salable business from the beginning, helped me build and design a powerful money-making business of my own.

I was learning from the past, living in the present, and focusing on the end.

PART II
The Aloha Money
Machine Method

Step One: Focus On The End

S tep one is all about strategies before tactics. Small business owners have been known to hold the business so tightly, like a baby, they restrict its growth. They don't stop to think about their business surviving without them. Because of this and the fear of losing control, they don't delegate and never allow the business to fully develop. Growth is limited when entrepreneurs try to control every little detail of the business.

Setting goals—making $500,000 a year or expanding the business to another location—is wonderful, but you first need to focus on building a business that runs independently of the owner. The growth of the business is only achieved when you change your philosophy and see the business as a separate entity, free and independent of the owner. You know the old saying, "If you love something, set it free… if it doesn't come back, hunt it down and kill it."

Having a clear vision of where you are and where you want to go will give you clarity on how you run your business and ultimately how to build your own Aloha Money Machine.

The man who once owned the largest General Motors dealership in the world got his start in the car business. He moved to Hawaii, continuing with cars and became a millionaire. He then became a

Rich Grandfather standing in front of a map indicating all the businesses he owned around the world.

multimillionaire with different companies before branching out to make millions more. However, Rich Grandfather wasn't always rich.

Rich Grandfather was born on an old farm near Stony Creek in Melfort, Saskatchewan, Canada. At the time, Stony Creek was a remote town surrounded by endless wheat fields and oil rigs. The town was known for it's hot, dusty summers and seven months of snow and cold during the winters.

As a little boy, Rich Grandfather started his working career by cleaning the garage at his father's small dealership. At age thirteen, Rich Grandfather dropped out of school to work at his dad's car dealership full-time.

The family dealership was an extremely small dealership with one mechanic and service garage. The garage repaired cars and tractors, and the dealership sold used Chevys, Nash cars, and Case tractors. It was a hard life, but the family made the most of it.

As Rich Grandfather got older, his father taught him how to work on engines. He loved engines and thought that he had a future career as a mechanic, but his dad had other plans. His dad wanted him to know the ins and outs of the entire dealership, not just automobile repairs.

At age fifteen, his job as a mechanic changed to office administrator. During this time, his two brothers moved to California to seek out their own opportunities working as car salesmen, leaving Rich Grandfather, the oldest son, at home.

Rich Grandfather now spent his days answering the phone, filing paperwork, and analyzing profit-and-loss statements. When he got a good understanding of profits and losses, his dad moved him from the office to sales and management.

Although his dad wanted him to learn everything about the auto dealership, he really wanted his son to understand the direction of his business. His dad was a firm believer that he could learn everything about the auto dealership, but he would fail unless he knew the direction of his business.

Although his dad didn't have much money and paid him little, he did encourage his son to reach for the stars and focus on the future. At an early age, his dad gave him a compass to keep track of his direction and introduced him to the business compass.

The Gift Of The Compass

At age thirteen, shortly after dropping out of school to work at the dealership full-time, Rich Grandfather's dad gave him a silver pocket compass that would change his business direction forever. On the back of the compass, the words *Business Compass* were engraved in the shiny silver.

If you want to be successful, you need to pay attention to the money and the direction of the business. Like a racecar, it's important to always look ahead of the curve and focus on where you want to go. The same rules apply in business: Knowing where you are in business is the first step, but focusing on where you want to go will ultimately give you business success.

If you lose focus on the direction you want to go, you can possibly crash or even lose track of the finish line. But, focusing on where you want to go on a daily basis will help you achieve your goal.

Most people don't ask for what they want because they don't know what they want. They can't envision the perfect business, because they don't know what it looks like. But men and women of vision can see the future and focus on what is most important for the directions they want to go. They can look at the future and paint the picture in their minds of what they want and what they need to build the perfect business. Like Picasso, who could see the image of his painting in his mind before he even started the work, business owners have to take the same approach and envision the future of their business. The compass allowed Rich Grandfather to stay focused.

The points on the business compass follow those hands of a standard compass, starting with *E* (Employee business), then *S* (Self business), then *W* (We business) and finally, *N* (Noble business). Just as the compass allowed ancient mariners to navigate uncharted waters, even when clouds covered the stars, a Business Compass allows business owners to navigate uncharted business waters, even when the way to do so is unclear. It allows you to learn from the past, live in the present, and focus on the end.

To understand the business compass, you must first understand the money in each of the four business types. All business is connected to money, and understanding the money will help you determine what business you're in. Business income is essential to all business, as consistent income will determine business survival. Taxes, payroll, utilities, and supplies do not compare to the importance of business income. Once you understand that money is the primary element of all business, you can make decisions more efficiently, no matter what business you are in. Money is not, as people often misquote, the root of all evil. It's *lack of money* that is the root of all evil, and the reason so many businesses fail.

Rich Grandfather's dad believed if you're an employee (*E*-business), you're in business to make someone else's company money. If you don't understand that the success of your career is determined by how much value or money you bring to the company, you will not truly succeed in the *E*-business. Similar to the *E*-business is the *S*-business (Self-employed), in which you trade time for dollars. The value in this business is determined by how much you work. If you do not work, you do not get paid. This is the main reason most S-business fail in the first five years of business.

However, the real magic is in the We-business.

The We-business is where most get rich and where Rich Grandfather built his empire. The We-business is all about hiring the right people, creating systems, and building a business that can survive without you. In the We-business, your success is determined by how much money your business makes regardless of the owner's involvement. In the We-business, you are not limited to what you can and cannot do physically, as you are free to use your time in the highest and best use. Unlike the S-business, where you must show up to get paid, you are free of that responsibility in the We-business.

As for the N-business, this is what Rich Grandfather would work his whole life to achieve.

Rich Grandfather believed the *N* in the compass represented *Noble*. Noble-Business was reserved for the ultra rich who make money with their money. Rich Grandfather's goal was to make $100 million (that amount would have made him a billionaire today) and live off the interest in a low-risk investment. In his mind, this was the noblest business of all.

Once he had a net worth of $100 million, Rich Grandfather believed he could retire and join the elite class of the noble rich. Although this was an impressive goal, he also had another reason for wanting to join the noble rich. More than anything, he wanted respect from those with incredible amounts of money. He wanted to prove to these people that he was equal, if not better, as he was self-made. He believed that once he achieved noble-rich status, people of wealth would respect him for achieving such an incredible goal.

Rich Grandfather's goal from the very start was to create a business of value that could be sold. Although he didn't sell every business he owned, he did have a clear vision of creating a business that had value. In his mind, a business of value was simply a business that investors wanted to buy. Investors were not interested in buying a job or working eight hours a day; they were only interested in buying cash flow investments. Knowing what investors wanted helped him make decisions that added value to the business on a daily basis.

Rich Grandfather focused on the direction of his business. He also followed the money, which is the subject of the next chapter.

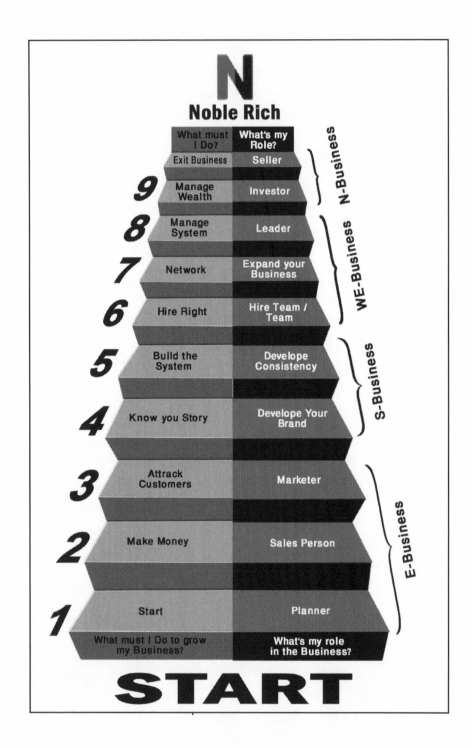

Step Two: Follow The Money

The Aloha Money Machine is designed like a real machine. Rich Grandfather and machines always understood each other. He fell in love the first time he spotted a tractor in his father's dealership. As a boy, he displayed an uncanny ability to size up any mechanism.

"I don't know why," Rich Grandfather said in a 1967 *Forbes* magazine interview, "but I've just always been able to size things up fast and to estimate values, even on machines I know nothing about and have never seen before."[7]

Rich Grandfather understood that if he was going to accomplish his goal of a net worth of $100 million, he would need to deconstruct business like a mechanic deconstructs an engine. He would first start with the power source of the business. What made the engine move? He found with the help of his business compass that the main source of power would come from business income, or revenue.

Grandfather found out quickly that business income was the best place to start as he thought about excelling in his career. Although his father owned the dealership, there was no handout or sympathy; if he wanted to excel in his career, he would have to figure out the most efficient way to add value to the company. It didn't take long to

---

[7] "Honolulu Horse Trader," *Forbes* magazine, July 1967.

realize that if he helped the company make money, he would earn a promotion, and this is exactly what he focused on.

In order to make the dealership more money, he would first need to understand where the dealership made the majority of its money. So, Rich Grandfather researched the business's lineage of sales to determine what product or service made the business the most money.

Did the majority of money come from automobile sales, from the garage, or from car loans? The Murphy family saw the importance of teaching their children all aspects of business, and Rich Grandfather was not excluded from learning everything there was to learn about the dealership. During his time as an office administrator he'd had an opportunity to understand what products or services netted the dealership the biggest return on investment, and he could then focus his time selling these specific products. During his investigation, Rich Grandfather had found the dealership made the most money from used car sales. If you've ever had your car worked on at a dealership, you may find that last sentence hard to believe, but it's true. Just like craps, poker and blackjack have the best "return on investment" in a casino for a gambler, used car sales have the best ROI for a car dealership.

Once he understood the primary income source (used car sales), he next wanted to understand where that business was generated: Who actually bought used cars, and where did these customers come from?

Looking at the history of past customers who had purchased used vehicles, he identified four core lead sources that served as pillars in the business. The first lead generator was the dealership's database of past clients; the second was mailers that the dealership sent out to the surrounding neighbors in the community. The third was local newspaper and radio advertising (there was no internet at the time). The last lead source was cold calling.

Once he understood his four pillars of lead generation, he then committed to one primary lead source to attract new leads. In the beginning, he found that the dealership database did not work, as past customers only wanted to work with the salesman they knew, and they didn't know Rich Grandfather yet. Advertising also did not work; he didn't have a budget or money to pay for leads. Although cold calling was the least-favorite lead generation method among the sales team, he would find that this was the best way to grow his own network. I know that sounds odd now, in this day and age of Caller ID, "Scam Likely" and spam call blocking apps; but back then the phone was still something of a modern marvel, and when it rang, you picked it up.

On a normal day, salesmen were known to sit around and wait for customers to show up. But Rich Grandfather was different. He took a proactive approach to sales that was unique at the time. He understood that the number one action he could do to increase the company's income and eventually get a promotion was to talk to quality leads. All other actions paled in comparison to this one simple task. This one action—simply talking to leads—was the very best way to increase revenue in the business.

Cold calling was difficult at first until he discovered a resource where he could buy a list of phone numbers at a very reasonable cost: a bank. The bank provided phone numbers of borrowers with recently paid-off and delinquent loans. Once he had this list of qualified leads, he then called these people on a regular basis—not to sell a vehicle, but to make an appointment. He understood the likelihood that someone would buy a car over the phone was very low. That is why he only focused on setting an appointment during the first conversation. He was more likely to make a sale if a customer met with him face to face. In the end he would learn that he could build a good business with warm leads, but an empire with cold leads.

Rich Grandfather did such an excellent job generating new leads that he was promoted to sales manager in one year. As sales manager, he would go on to teach his team the system for generating and tracking leads. Dialing for dollars in the automobile sales business was born.

To illustrate the concept, the system went something like the following.

Rich Grandfather determined that it would take around fifty calls to set five appointments. Out of the five people who set appointments, three would eventually buy. Once he had this general calculation, he then set a weekly goal for each salesman to sell six cars per week. To meet this productivity quota, each salesman was required to call and track 100 conversations a week.

100 calls = ten appointments

Ten appointments = six car sales

Setting a goal to call 100 people a week greatly increased the salesmen's income and the overall revenue of the dealership.

Rich Grandfather noticed the importance of teaching his team the secrets of following the money. He taught his employees the secrets of his success as a former salesman so they could become successful on their own. As a result, the company's sales increased. At seventeen years old, he was next promoted to general manager and was responsible for the entire dealership, including the garage. Although the dealership was small this was a huge achievement for a seventeen year old.

As Rich Grandfather's income increased, he remained disciplined and continued to save a percentage of his gross income (my recommendation is to follow the practice I did: Pay yourself first and save at least 10 percent for growing your business). His plan was to save a percentage of every dollar he earned until he had enough money to start his own dealership. Because he was able to limit his spending and save a percentage of his gross income, he eventually had enough money to finally open his own business.

He continued to learn everything he could about running an automobile dealership but paid close attention to the direction of his business compass. He also paid attention to the people who were making the most money. He found that the people who were making the most money were the people who owned dealerships in the S-businesses and We-businesses. After years learning everything he could about running an auto dealership, it was now time for him to make a move and open a business of his own. Only a few short years after starting as a general manager, he was ready to open his own dealership.

Once he understood the direction of his business and where the money came from, he could then move his investigation to understand the third part of his formula, which was understanding his customers: the subject of the next chapter.

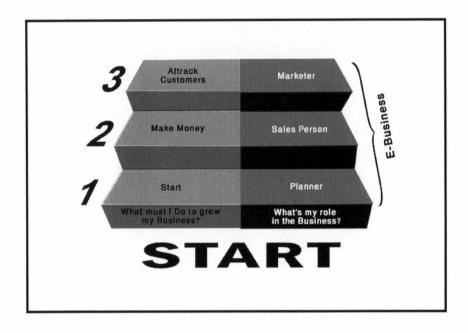

Step Three: Attract Customers

R ich Grandfather made the conscious decision never again to be an employee and to focus his sights on the S-business. He had always wanted to own a business and now was the time. Although he was excited to finally start his own business, he also knew that he would have a problem: the same problem that most businesses face when they start out. He would have a hard time attracting new customers, especially in a new area. So, instead of taking the old approach and marketing to everyone, he would take a new approach and market to a specific target audience. As you often hear in the public speaking business, "the riches are in the niches." Or, more appropriately for the automobile sales business, "pick a lane."

Rich Grandfather would have appreciated the adage:

Stop chasing new business and start attracting it.

He knew if he understood his true customer (today, some say *target audience*), he could eliminate most of the marketing and simply place his business in a location where his ideal customer was. Ask yourself, "Who is my ideal customer?" Instead of his customer coming to him, he would go to his customer. To understand his customer in depth, he would have to ask himself three questions:

What business am I in? Who is likely to buy from me? What do my customers consider valuable?

He would first look at what he was selling to answer the question, what business am I in? During his time in the E-business as general manager, he noticed that the dealership made more money on the sale of commercial trucks versus cars, as the wholesale cost was much lower at the time. If he were to achieve his dream of entering the noble rich, he would have to sell high-ticket items that netted him the highest return on the sale.

Once he made the decision to sell commercial trucks, he then tried his best to answer the second question: Who is my customer? He concluded that the people who bought commercial trucks were business owners: specifically, business owners who needed to transport goods and services from location to location. These included farming, shipping, manufacturing, and service businesses.

Farming and agricultural businesses were especially interesting to Rich Grandfather, as he understood these customers. He had personally grown up on a farm, worked on tractors, and understood what farmers needed to be successful. Since the seventh grade, three of the best years of his life, after he'd quit school to work at his father's dealership, had been spent analyzing the farming and agricultural customer. He had to know everything he could about his customers to win the sale. He wanted to know how old the average customers were; what percentage were first-generation farmers? He wanted to know how much money they made and the average size of their farms. His goal was to understand his target audience's buying habits to give them exactly what they wanted, and this information would eventually pay off.

Although it would have been easy to open a dealership the next town over from his father's dealership, he also knew the importance of locating his target audience. Rich Grandfather was methodical in the process of finding the perfect location to start his business. He spent months researching his target audience. He researched different communities, cities, and even different countries. He wanted to be in an area with low competition and maximum potential for growth. His plan was to open his business in the middle of a growing community where his ideal customer congregated.

Two months after Rich Grandfather's decision to start his own business, he finally got his big break. He read in a trade magazine that multiple trucks where being shipped directly from the manufacturer to a small town in California. He would find out through additional research that large canneries were suddenly opening in the San Joaquin Valley, as farm production had grown tremendously due to new water irrigation canals in the area. Because of these canals, farmers had more fresh fruit and vegetables than they could immediately sell, and there was a serious need to transport these fruits before they spoiled. Rich Grandfather knew that those farms and canneries would need some way to transport their goods. Demand meet supply, supply meet demand.

With this information Rich Grandfather decided to take the leap of faith and open his first business in a new location, new area, and new country. With this decision and an understanding of his target audience, he quit his father's dealership, packed up all his belongings, and moved from Canada to the United States. He would eventually land in Manteca, California, about fifty miles east of San Francisco.

Although he was fearful of failure, he was also excited to sell commercial trucks to business owners, as it would give him a chance to network with successful people. He loved talking business, but more importantly, he loved talking to successful business owners. He also liked the fact that there was little emotion in this type of sale. If a business owner needed a work truck for business, there was little negotiation on price and very little feeling in the transaction. Also, business owners were known to buy multiple trucks at a time to equip their growing businesses.

With the money he had saved working at his father's dealership, Rich Grandfather opened his very own Chevrolet dealership selling commercial trucks in California. Because he had spent the time to understand his customer, he was able to answer the third question: What do my customers consider valuable?

Rich Grandfather understood if he were ever going to be successful in selling commercial trucks, he would have to help other business owners become successful. He had faith that if he helped enough business owners succeed, he would succeed himself. There are two main factors all business owners value more than anything. The first thing they value is time, and the second is money; Rich Grandfather understood and respected this fact. His customers wanted a fair deal when they purchased commercial vehicles, and they wanted a quick sale to save time.

Rich Grandfather gave them fair deals. He bought in bulk from the manufacturer. Because he bought in bulk, he was able to buy at a discount and pass the savings to his customers. Although buying in bulk limited the selection, he did have three models of trucks his customers could pick from. By offering his customers a platinum, gold and silver package, he limited the decision-making process and ultimately moved more units.

The second factor his customers valued was time. Rich Grandfather made every attempt to get his customer a truck as soon as possible because he understood that time was money. If no truck were available, he loaned his future customers a brand-new truck at no charge to accommodate their deliveries. He went out of his way to help his customers, as he knew that a satisfied customer is a repeat customer.

Every business has a target audience. The better we understand our customer and target audience, the more likely we will be successful in building the Aloha Money Machine.

Knowing the trends that influence customers also helps us to anticipate our clients' needs before the competition. Understanding and anticipating his clients' future needs contributed to Rich Grandfather's success. He also knew how to craft the right story, which is the subject of the next chapter.

Step Four: Craft Your Story

After two years in business, Rich Grandfather's dealership was profitable. He was selling trucks, building his client database, and life was good. He had a brand-new dealership with his name on the building; he had employees, a wife, and two babies at home. It was the first time in his life that he was pleased.

Little did he know, during this time he was learning the secrets to building the Aloha Money Machine formula. As he refined the system, he was eventually able to make the switch from S-business to We-business. He changed his philosophy and built a business that ran independently of himself.

With the success of the Manteca truck dealership, he now had plans to expand his business by opening multiple locations around the country to provide multiple streams of income to achieve his lifelong goal of entering the noble-rich.

Everything Changed

Because of Rich Grandfather's methodical approach to starting a new business, he sold an unprecedented number of commercial trucks in the Manteca and San Francisco area, but while his sales were impressive, his timing was disastrous.

In 1929, the U.S. economy fell through the floor. It was the worst financial depression in American history. Desperation was now the new land Rich Grandfather had inherited.

In October 1929, the American stock market crashed, and with it, hard times came to California, the country, and the world. For millions of people and for businesses, fear and failure were now commonplace, as hundreds of thousands of Americans lost their homes and farms. The 1930s emerged to be a gloomy time as the Great Depression took hold. People were out of work, standing in bread lines, and living on the streets. People had no money to buy food, let alone new trucks. Profits made during the roaring twenties seemed to disappear overnight, and many dealerships, including Rich Grandfather's, didn't weather the storm. Grandfather lost everything: his dealership, his cars, his home, and his money. The Great Depression left him, his wife, and his two children broke and bankrupt. The next few years were a dark and dismal time for them.

At rock bottom and penniless, his luck would change once again as he would bump into a man who would give him hope. Before the Depression, this man had worked for Rich Grandfather as a mechanic. The mechanic explained that he had previously worked in Honolulu, and Hawaii was one of the few places that had work. He said that more and more people were moving to Hawaii. In an interview for the *Regina Leader-Post*, Rich Grandfather explained, "He sold me on Hawaii." With a wife, two small children, $4,000 in debts, and $20 in his pocket, Rich Grandfather spent the last of his money on a boarding pass to Hawaii.

The journey from California to Hawaii at the time required four days of travel across the Pacific Ocean by boat. His wife wondered what they would do when they got to Hawaii, as they couldn't afford a place to live, let alone having money to open a car dealership. They barely had enough money for the boat ride. But Rich Grandfather was confident. He had a secret weapon. He'd grown up poor with limited resources and knew what it would take to attract business.

Although times where tough, Rich Grandfather was confident in his secret weapon: his business story. He knew that his business story would attract the right target audience and help him get work at a dealership. Although he was broke, he still had his business story and used it to market himself to the right people. His business story was simple, easy to understand and remember.

"My name is George Murphy. I'm a successful auto dealer. Before the depression I ran a dealership called Murphy Motors after my own name. I work with people who want to start dealerships and people who want to grow their auto dealerships. In fact, I started working in a car dealership when I was five years old and have never looked back. When you've run a car dealership successfully for as many years as I have, you can run any business. I have worked as a mechanic, sales manager, and a general manager. I know everything there is to know about car dealerships."

Once he added credibility to his story, he then added value with something similar to the words, "My past employers would tell you that my knowledge of dealerships brought them more focus on a daily basis, which attracted more customers, stimulated more referrals, and ultimately generated more money. On a personal note, I have big dreams of becoming a successful rancher one day and own several hundred head of cattle."

The Formula:

1. Your name: George Murphy
2. Accomplishments (I'm a successful auto dealer or author of a book)

3. Company you work for or worked for in the past. (Murphy Motors)

4. Your target audience (Dealership owners)

5. Credibility statement (What makes you an expert)

6. What are the results people have when working with you? (More customers, referrals, and money)

7. Personal story (Something to keep the conversation going, Rich Grandfather always wanted to own a cattle ranch.)

The ancient Greek philosopher Plato once said, "Those who tell the story rule society." The most critical aspect, and possibly the hardest thing to do in business, is to tell a compelling story. The business story is the foundation for building a brand. Branding is all about defining you, finding your voice, and leadership style, no matter where you are on the business compass. To tell a compelling business story, you need to get people interested and excited about what you do, and more importantly, what you can do for them. The person with the freshest story will always get the business.

Rich Grandfather was well rehearsed on his business story. He recited his business story back to himself several times throughout the day until he could recite the words forward and backward. Because of his confidence in his business story, he quickly landed a job in Hawaii making $39.00 a week selling Fords at Universal Motors in Honolulu.

Hawaii was everything he had heard about; the opportunity was endless. New construction and development were everywhere, military outposts were being built, harbors were being constructed, and restaurants and stores were being developed. There were also plenty of jobs at sugar cane plantations. The word about Hawaii's growth traveled quickly, with more and more people moving to Hawaii for opportunity.

An employee once again, Rich Grandfather knew that if he made his boss look good, he, too, would look good and eventually be promoted. Rich Grandfather understood that the secret to success in the E-business is helping the business succeed, and that is exactly what he did. If car sales needed to increase, so that his boss could receive his yearly bonus, Rich Grandfather would do everything he could to increase the company's sales. In return, he quickly climbed the corporate ladder and became indispensable to his boss and the company's success.

Rich Grandfather added an incredible amount of value to Universal Motors. Because of this, he was promoted to sales manager after a year of employment. Although the sales manager position was great, he really wanted to be the general manager. As general manager he would be the highest paid employee the dealership had.

In 1937 Rich Grandfather did, in fact, become general manager of Universal Motors. As general manager, he was officially the highest paid employee and now responsible for the entire dealership.

Some people work their whole lives to hold the title of general manager, but once again, he was not satisfied. Although Rich Grandfather had an attractive salary and a stable career, he still looked at his business compass on a daily basis and envisioned himself moving from E-business (employee business) to S-business (self business) and opening his own business once again. He knew that the only way that he could achieve his dream of becoming rich and achieving noble-rich status is if he owned his own business.

In preparation to start his next business, Rich Grandfather would have to change his business story to reflect his expertise: He would have to switch emphasis from running others' businesses to running his own business. Understanding both the money part of the business and customer part of the business helped him crafted the perfect new business story. The business story was the backbone of his marketing efforts and ultimately helped him start his next business.

Business partners, employees, and customers all need to be able to accurately tell others what they do. If business owners can clarify what precisely they do and whom they serve, they can drastically grow their business. When you can answer the simple question, "What do you do" in a brief and easy-to-understand way, you will attract more customers and reach a deeper level with existing customers.

At the height of his career, Rich Grandfather was known as the person who made businesses profitable.

He was so clear about his business story that everyone around him knew exactly what he did. He would say with confidence, "I buy businesses in the red (failing) and sell them in the black (profitable)." It was simple and easy to understand; people from around the world would give Rich Grandfather opportunities that were not offered to the public. People sought him out as the man known for turning failing businesses around.

Once he defined his business story as a man who turned failing businesses around for a profit, he had more business than he could handle. His business story also helped him attract some of the sharpest and brightest employees in the world. These people wanted to work for him because his business story was so convincing they believed he had the knowledge to make them rich.

But more is needed than a compelling story. Rich Grandfather learned you need a system too, which is the subject of the next chapter.

7

Step Five: Build The System

Although Rich Grandfather had lost everything in the Great Depression, he believed that if his system was strong, he could reinvent his business model once again. Before Rich Grandfather lost his dealership due to the Great Depression, his biggest lesson came from a man looking to buy Rich Grandfather's first dealership in California.

It was a beautiful day in sunny California, and business for Rich Grandfather was good. His employees were busy helping customers, and cash was rolling in. The man who came in that day resembled a rich cowboy and drove a brand-new white convertible Cadillac. He was wearing a tailored brown suit, bolo tie, and a cowboy hat. Rich Grandfather would wear a similar outfit later in life. The man asked to see the owner of the dealership, and Rich Grandfather greeted him in the lobby.

The man in the cowboy hat looked at Grandfather, smiled and said, "I know you, boy, but the last time I saw you, you were working for a small dealership in Canada." He was a man who had encouraged Grandfather to open his own dealership back when he was seventeen years old, working at his father's dealership.

The man in the cowboy hat said, "It looks like you took my advice and opened your own business. You have done well, and you have

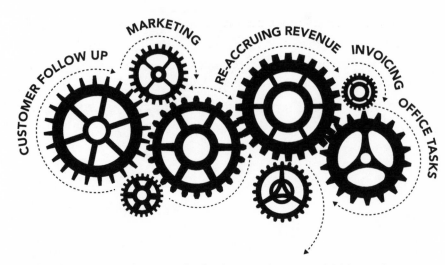

built a business to be proud of. That is why I would like to buy your dealership from you." He pulled out his checkbook. "How much do you want for your dealership, boy? Please understand, I can pay you in one lump sum or pay you throughout the course of five years if you don't feel like paying the capital gains tax all at once," he said as he laughed. "I will write you a deposit for the business right now to show you that I'm serious, and we can settle the rest later," the man in the cowboy hat said.

Rich Grandfather looked down at the blank check and then slowly raised his head.

"My dealership is not for sale," Rich Grandfather said.

But the man insisted, saying, "I buy profitable businesses, and it looks like your dealership is profitable. I will make you an offer today based on the salability of your business."

Rich Grandfather found the word *salability* fascinating.

"What do you mean, salability?" Grandfather said.

"Son, I buy businesses that generate consistent cash flow each month. I can determine the salability of your business based on how many car loans you own. I can also predict the salability of business by determining how much recurring revenue you make on a consistent basis. I factor in your monthly net income from car sales and loans minus expenses, but most importantly, the salability of your business is based on several months of consistent cash flow.

"If your business generates consistent monthly cash flow, I will buy you out right now or pay you a salary for the rest of your life. Son, you won't have to work another day of your life," the man in the cowboy hat said, with a big smile.

Rich Grandfather thought about the proposal: Not working another day in his life? But he was curious about how the dealership would operate without him. Grandfather asked, "Wouldn't you need me to continue working until you found a suitable replacement for me before you completely bought me out? Surely you couldn't do what I do on a daily basis to keep the dealership positive."

The man in the cowboy hat looked at Grandfather and laughed, "Son, I know your business better then you do. I have a business system to take ownership of this dealership right away. I have a team of people I can bring in from my other dealerships to analyze your systems and determine what is working and what is not working."

The man in the cowboy hat continued. "After they analyze your strengths and primary source of income, we can then understand its weaknesses to improve it. We can develop systems to give your customers exactly what they want. I will streamline your business to become a cash flow powerhouse.

"I also have some of the best managers money can buy. They will come in here, clean house, and get your employees to follow my proven system for doing business. They will train your existing managers to follow my business system or hire new managers if they can't keep up. And the best part is, your customers will love the change and be glad you sold. Your customers will love the consistency of my business system. People love a business that is consistent; they love knowing that they will get the same experience year after year. They also love that we build relationships with our customers and mail them car maintenance reminders and birthday cards every year. My system is so good that I don't personally have to be here once the system is in place. I can focus my attention on what makes me the most money."

Grandfather replied, "If you don't mind my asking, what makes you the most money?"

The man in the cowboy hat said. "Well, son, I've found that I make the most money from buying salable businesses just like yours. I focus on either failing companies or business with the potential for future growth. The best use of my time is researching businesses for sale and talking to owners of profitable businesses, like you. Networking with entrepreneurs like yourself is the highest use of my time, which makes me the most money in the long run," he said.

Although the idea of getting a monthly salary for the rest of his life was appealing, Rich Grandfather knew that he would never accomplish his goal of entering the ranks of the noble-rich if he sold. He never lost focus on his dream of becoming a millionaire. Because of this, he didn't sell that day. But this conversation opened his eyes to the importance of building a money-making system. If Rich Grandfather were to be rich, he would have to follow in the footsteps of the rich cowboy and build a salable business with consistent cash flow. He would have to give his customers the service they deserved systematically. He also realized that he would have to develop a system of experts instead of being the only expert. He understood that if he were going to create a salable business, he would have to fine-tune the business system to generate consistent cash flow. Once he was able to do this, he could then use his time more efficiently. The point is business consistency greatly increases the value of a business and ultimately attracts investors.

Develop The System

If the fuel to the Aloha Money Machine is money, then the engine in the Aloha Money Machine is the system. Once Rich Grandfather understood the importance of stabilizing his income through recurring revenue, he then looked for additional ways to make consistent money on a regular basis. One of these consistent streams of income would be issuing car loans, collecting checks from borrowers making monthly car payments. These consistent payments would be predictable, stable, and would occur monthly, at a relatively high degree of certainty.

Throughout his years at the dealership, Rich Grandfather created many systems for completing daily tasks. One of these systems was a process for selling loans that consistently closed sales. Although I couldn't find the exact system Rich Grandfather used for selling loans, I did research several profitable dealerships. In my investigation, I found a dealership in Oceanside, California, which had a similar system for consistently closing loans.

The dealer in Oceanside (who didn't want to be named in the interview) was an older gentleman in his seventies who had more than forty years of experience. He was an interesting character who spent most of his days attending car auctions and meeting employees. He was also financially free; he had "consistent cash flow and time to enjoy it." I would find out that he, too, had adopted a philosophy of building a system around stabilizing income. In a raspy voice, he broke down his process and explained his own six-step system for selling car loans.

The Six-Step Oceanside System For Selling Automobile Loans

Step One: The first step, he said, is to *gather information*. In order for a customer to get a loan, the dealership needs to collect some personal information from the customer. Customers are instructed to fill out a document at the front desk. This document includes personally identifying information, employment history, and living expenses to determine credit default risk. The document also asks the customer to include birth dates and favorite restaurants. Once this information is filled out, it is handed off to an assistant, who directs the customer to a loan officer.

Step 2: This is the *get-to-know-the-customer* step, intended to connect to the customers on a personal level. The loan officer's goal is to get to know the customer during this conversation and is instructed to use the second document in the system for selling car loans. Here, the officer asks the customer a series of questions about what they are looking for in a car. Although the approved loan amount will ultimately determine the kind of car customers can afford, customers themselves do appreciate this conversation, as it makes them feel heard and respected. After five minutes of conversation, the assistant at the front desk who collected document one is instructed to provide the customers with their favorite beverage. (This information was asked and provided during step one, coffee, tea, or soda, floor mats, undercoating, or extended warranty).

Step Three: The *added-value* conversation step. In this step, the loan officer adds credibility and value for the borrower by explaining a series of bullet points that explain the benefits of using the dealerships loan services versus those of an outside company, including examples of past satisfied customers.

Step Four: Let's call this the *explain-the-product* step, the old man said. Loan officers are instructed to provide three different documents with loan options. Each document included colorful charts with easy-to-understand payment plans. The charts are designed to help customers choose a loan option from the three plans. During this time, the assistant is instructed to provide refills to the customer's favorite beverage based on the document originally filled out in step one.

Step Five: In this step, the loan officer *reviews the product and answers the customer's questions*. This step is designed to explain the contract to the customer. The loan officer is well trained to answer primarily from a large bank of memorized, scripted answers and to expect difficult questions.

Step Six: The last step is called *close the sale and follow-up*. Once the customer signs the contract, a salesperson is instructed to congratulate the customer on the new purchase and hand them the keys. The loan officer is then instructed to enter the customer name and loan information into the dealership's loan system. The loan officer is also instructed to enter the customer's birthday and loan anniversary into the dealership's master calendar and database. Based on the information entered during step one, the dealership then mails birthday cards as well as annual gift certificates to the borrower's favorite restaurant every anniversary of the purchase of their new car. This practice increased customer loyalty, the old man said.

Once the system was created, the Oceanside dealer taught all of his employees the individual steps to learn the system. "Although some of my employees have a difficult time adjusting to the system at first, they learn to appreciate the system, because it produces consistent sales," this experienced dealership owner told me. "Customers also appreciate the system. It is organized, easy to understand, and consistent. Customers would have appreciated the higher level of service in your Grandfather's dealership, as well," the old man reflected.

In the end, customers did consistently buy vehicles and refinanced their loans through Rich Grandfather's dealership, and they did it year after year. Implementing a recurring revenue system guaranteed stability, predictability, and a high customer lifetime value (CLV).

Without a system, the business becomes unpredictable and unreliable. But the best part of the system is that the owner does not have to be involved in every sale, as the system can be taught to employees. Rich Grandfather was successful, as he built a system for his employees to follow and managed the system, not the employee. He also held his employees accountable for following the system.

After you have the system in place, you need to focus on hiring the right employees to run the system, which is the subject of the next chapter.

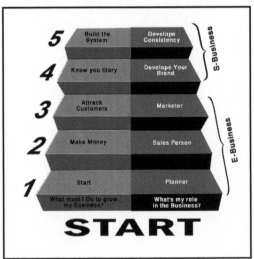

8

Step Six: Hire Right

J ust one year after becoming general manager of Universal Motors, Rich Grandfather would make a move from E-business to S-business once again. Seven years after moving to Hawaii dead broke and bankrupt, Grandfather would climb out of poverty. Once again, he had followed the strategy of saving 10 percent of everything he made working at Universal Motors until he had enough cash to buy his very own car dealership.

In 1938, Rich Grandfather bought a run-down dealership with plans to turn it into a successful business. He would enter the S-business and sell Oldsmobiles on the island of Honolulu. Rich Grandfather was proud of his accomplishment and once again characteristically renamed the dealership Murphy Motors after himself. He loved seeing his name on the side of the building, and more importantly, he loved proving people wrong. For the second time in his life, he would crawl out of the slums of poverty and show those who had doubted him that he could become successful through business. They say that living well is the best revenge. I believe that the best revenge is living well above your doubters' low expectations.

Although Rich Grandfather had a system for growing his new dealership, he didn't have employees to run the system. He knew that the machine would only work if he hired the right people to grow his business. With the goal of growing his business, he would focus on hiring an all-star sales team.

Throughout Rich Grandfather's entire career, he was always known to hire the best of the best. He did this by understanding personality types to place the right person in the right position. For Rich Grandfather, it wasn't as important to hire the most educated or polished as it was to hire people who connected well with others. It was equally important that these people thought highly of themselves and would not give up in the face of adversity. He was more concerned with the ability to connect with people to find out their personality type than researching their pedigrees.

During interviews, he would ask employment candidates about their childhoods and other personal questions to determine their personality types. When hiring salespeople, his goal was to get to know them personally; then he would attack. He would say something to the effect of, "I don't think you're the right person for the job. I only have one job opening, and I really don't think it is the right fit for you." He added this statement to his interviews to test the potential sales person's resilience. If the interviewee caved and finished the interview with "OK, well, thank you for your time," then Rich Grandfather knew that he was speaking to the wrong person for the job. But if the interviewee said something like, "In my last job, I outsold 90 percent of all my coworkers, and most of them had more experience than me," Rich Grandfather knew that he had someone who would fight to make the sale.

Ultimately he wanted someone who could connect with others, but who would not give up under pressure—someone who was driven to make the sale would ultimately grow the company's income.

Because Rich Grandfather hired the all-star salespeople, he quickly turned the run-down dealership into a profitable small business. But he had a problem: this dealership was small, with limited advertising exposure and inventory space. He was losing business. His customers were going to other dealerships with better locations and a larger inventory. Apparently, sometimes size *does* matter.

Although Rich Grandfather finally had his own dealership, he was not happy with his present circumstances. He knew that if he were ever going to become rich from business, he would have to market to a larger audience and give his customers what they wanted. To do this, he needed to offer his customers something unique, increase his inventory, and hire more employees.

Rich Grandfather was now on the hunt to purchase raw land with high visibility and greater space for inventory. His goal was to expand his car inventory by becoming the main General Motors (GM) distributor on the island.

However he had two more problems: he didn't have enough money to purchase the land, let alone build a new dealership, and the huge corporation of General Motors was not interested in going into business with a small-time dealer. Rich Grandfather knew that he had to do something to gain the respect of GM, and he also needed to attract a team of partners who would finance the purchase of the property. To address these challenges, he switched gears from hiring the best employees to attracting the best partners.

Growing The Team

Rich Grandfather developed a plan to stand out from his competition and do what he did best, which was attracting the kind of people he needed. He knew that the personality type of an investor would want to know that Rich Grandfather was credible and a good investment.

So he made a plan to market his *personal brand and credibility* to a select group. He would do this by advertising. His plan was to advertise his business story of a successful auto dealer to gain credibility.

He raised his profile by advertising in an article that read:

> *Murphy is president and general manager of Murphy Motors Ltd. To which position he brings along experience in various fields, and he has a high standing both as a successful merchandiser of automotive equipment and as an executive in charge of business affairs.*[8]

This publicity gave him credibility with GM and his future financial partners. Shortly after this article was published, Rich Grandfather would go into business with both GM and two money partners with plans to construct the most significant car dealership in all of Hawaii.

Grandfather would announce in the *Honolulu Star-Bulletin* on July 23, 1939: "We are now planning a building with approximately 40,000 square feet of floor space. This building will incorporate the very latest ideas both for the display of passenger cars and trucks and for complete service. That is a very definite part of our program."[9]

With the help of two money partners and the contract awarded from GM, Rich Grandfather opened the doors to his brand-new dealership, called "Aloha Motors," selling Chevrolets and GM products. Aloha Motors was in the middle of Waikiki, in one of the busiest areas in all of Hawaii. Waikiki was thriving. Its location was near Pearl Harbor, hotels, restaurants, the airport, and of course, the beautiful white sand beaches. At the time, this was the center of new development

---

[8] "Former Melfort...Murphy Motors Organised; Major Step in Auto Field," *Melfort Journal,* July 12, 1938, p. 2.

[9] *Honolulu Star-Bulletin.* July 23, 1939

and growth in Honolulu. It was the busiest location in all of Hawaii; in fact, to this day it still is the busiest location in all of Hawaii. To get an idea of the size and magnitude of the dealership, Aloha Motors was located at the same place where today the 1.1-million-square-foot Honolulu Convention Center stands today. This piece of land is now some of the most valuable real estate in all of Hawaii.

With this newfound exposure, enormous inventory, and service center, Rich Grandfather was now on a path to grow his new team. He would focus his time on hiring the right salespeople and managers to run the system.

Sales are the lifeblood of business. But if you're not effective at converting leads into sales, you're wasting both time and money. To do this accurately requires great sales managers. But filling this role takes more than just promoting salespeople. It requires hiring the right personality types who are skilled at leading, nurturing, and bringing out the best in others.

(Although Rich Grandfather was extremely good at understanding personality types, it's not necessary that you have this natural ability. Today, it is easier than ever to understand the personalities of yourself and others by taking a personality assessment. There are many instruments that you can choose from, include DiSC, Myers-Briggs, the Winslow Personality Profile, and of course, a drug test. Well, you have to have a way to "weed" out the bad apples. You can research which makes the most sense for you. The advantage of the owner taking a personality test is that you may find out some interesting facts about yourself. Understanding your own personality might help you understand the best fit when hiring others. I had a client who wanted to grow his real estate brokerage; he hired five salespeople who were motivated, bright, and focused on the future.

Aerial view of the five-story racks at Aloha Motors. Aloha Motors, Inc., the largest Chevrolet-Oldsmobile Agency in the world, and the largest automobile agency in the Islands, Honolulu Star-Bulletin.

Unfortunately, the owner had the same personality, and because of this, sales did not increase. The owner didn't need more visionary leaders. He needed salespeople who would make the calls and close the deal. Once he understood the personality of salespeople, he fired the first five and hired people with the appropriate personalities who were motivated by cold-calling. As soon as he did this, his sales grew.) Ultimately, he would find out that he could build a good business with warm leads, but an empire with cold leads.

Because Rich Grandfather knew the importance of hiring the right people to run the different parts of the system, his new dealership was an instant success. However, even though his sales increased, times were tumultuous. Talks of war were on everyone's mind. Rich Grandfather's money partners were now getting nervous; they wanted to cash out and sell the "Aloha Motors" Money Machine.

In the previously referenced *Forbes* interview, Rich Grandfather said he didn't sell, but instead bought out his two partners' interest in Aloha Motors. "'I gave them their checks in my office, told them I thought they were foolish to sell, and that in a few short years we could all make millions,' he says, smiling. 'They sold anyway, and I made the millions.'"

After the sale, Rich Grandfather hired a truly talented marketing director who suggested installing a creative marketing display to increase inventory and boost sales.

After consideration, Grandfather took the advice of the marketing director and installed a huge, four-story parking elevator at the dealership. Customers could pick cars from a rack of vehicles, and an elevator would pick up the car and lower it to the ground. This was an impressive machine, and people from all around the island came to see this four-story car elevator. This machine greatly increased his marketing efforts. Rich Grandfather had invested a considerable amount in these auto elevators, and now he needed to purchase additional vehicles to fill his four-story parking racks.

The day he intended to order 100 more vehicles to expand his inventory was the same day that would be remembered in history. Grandfather's business would be changed forever: December 7, 1941. On that morning, hundreds of Japanese fighter planes would descend on Honolulu.

Pearl Harbor is a United States naval base located near the original Aloha Motors dealership and was the target of a devastating surprise attack by Japanese forces during World War II. Rich Grandfather witnessed the attack on Honolulu and remembers seeing Japanese fighters fly overhead on their way to Pearl Harbor.

It was 8:00 a.m. on a Sunday morning, and Grandfather remembers seeing planes fly overhead and noticed red dots on the wings. He immediately turned on the radio and listened carefully to hear what was going on; when he heard bombs and bullets raining down onto vessels moored at Pearl Harbor, he knew Hawaii was under attack. From the dealership, you had a clear view of the Japanese fighter planes that flew overhead and billows of black smoke filling the air around Pearl Harbor.

Explosions continued for the next few minutes, then suddenly stopped for a moment. At 8:10 a.m., the Japanese dropped a 1,800-pound bomb that smashed through the deck of the battleship USS Arizona. When the ship exploded, the blast was so loud that it shook Rich Grandfather's dealership more than ten miles away.

Less than two hours after the surprise attack by the Japanese, it was over. Nearly twenty naval vessels, including eight battleships and more than 300 airplanes, had been destroyed. More than 2,400 Americans had perished in the attack, including civilians, and another 1,000 people were severely wounded. The day after the assault, President Franklin D. Roosevelt asked Congress to declare war on Japan.

Rich Grandfather's dealership was about to change forever. From now on, networking would be critical to his business's success, which is the subject of the next chapter.

Honolulu Star-Bulletin 1st EXTRA

2 PAGES—HONOLULU, TERRITORY OF HAWAII, U.S.A., SUNDAY, DECEMBER 7, 1941—8 PAGES ★ PRICE FIVE CENTS

WAR!

(Associated Press by Transpacific Telephone)

SAN FRANCISCO, Dec. 7.—President Roosevelt announced this morning that Japanese planes had attacked Manila and Pearl Harbor.

OAHU BOMBED BY JAPANESE PLANES

SIX KNOWN DEAD, 21 INJURED, AT EMERGENCY HOSPITAL

Attack Made On Island's Defense Areas

Hundreds See City Bombed

Names of Dead and Injured

Schools Closed

Editorial

HAWAII MEETS THE CRISIS

BULLETIN

9

Step Seven: Networking Your Database

aking preparations to go to war, the United States was in panic and hysteria. It was a scary time, and the possibility that the Japanese would attack again was on everyone's mind. In Hawaii, there was a significant military presence even before the attack, and the people who lived on the island had felt protected, but after the attack, people felt frightened and vulnerable.

For Rich Grandfather, however, dark times equaled great opportunity. As quoted in the aforementioned *Forbes* magazine article, he said, "While everybody else was selling, I bought." The situation at the time was gray; the Japanese had just bombed Pearl Harbor, the world was at war, and life in Hawaii was now changed. People were focused on their current state, but Rich Grandfather saw past the present day and looked for opportunity in the future. He was learning from the past, living in the present, and focusing on the end, as always.

He wanted to be rich through business and knew this could be the opportunity he had been looking for. Much like the game of poker, you need to know when to hold them and when to fold them, and Rich Grandfather saw an opportunity to play his hand. He was all in. This was either going to make him or break him. But it was an opportunity he couldn't refuse.

Due to Hawaii's proximity to the Pacific and U.S. allies around the Pacific Rim, Hawaii became a melting pot of military personnel and residents. The economy in Hawaii saw sharp economic growth as more and more people were stationed in the islands. Businesses prospered for those who were directly associated with war efforts. The war would drive Hawaii's economy for the next several years.[10]

Throughout Rich Grandfather's business career, he always valued his little black book of contacts. He had an uncanny ability to keep track of people he thought might be of importance. He believed that the quickest way to become rich was through people. In business, he found the most valuable asset that he owned was this list. Diamonds were found in this list, and he held these contacts in the highest regard. In every business Rich Grandfather entered, he would gather contact information from people he associated with. Not only would he gather contact information from his customers, but also from people who could one day advance his career. Rich Grandfather would find out shortly how powerful this list would be.

The Second World War pitted two alliances against each other: the Axis powers and the Allied powers. The leading Axis powers were Germany, Italy, and Japan; the Allied powers were the United States, the United Kingdom, the Soviet Union, and China. The Allied powers would later band together with several smaller countries to form an international body that would eventually be known as the United Nations.[11]

---

[10] "Hawaii After Pearl Harbor," Visit Pearl Harbor, March 8, 2017, https://visitpearlharbor.org/hawaii-pearl-harbor/.

[11] "Cold War Foreign Policy," Stanford History Education Group, https://sheg.stanford.edu/history-assessments/cold-war-foreign-policy.

With the proximity of Hawaii to surrounding allied countries, Rich Grandfather had an opportunity to quickly grow his business. Although he originally thought he would become rich selling cars, he got his first real boost in the exporting business. Rich Grandfather found success importing and exporting to Allied countries as war efforts continued.

Soon, he was supplying cars and trucks to the whole Pacific Rim and the Far East. In 1942, one year after the attack on Pearl Harbor, Aloha Motors would become the largest General Motors dealership in the world.

Truck, cars, and General Motors products were imported to Hawaii, then shipped to Allied countries across the entire Pacific Rim. Rich Grandfather took full advantage of this opportunity and got a piece of all of it. Not only did he take advantage of the exporting business; he also took advantage of his database of contacts.

He had built an extensive network of high-ranking officials in Hawaii throughout the years, and now these officials needed to buy vehicles in bulk, but the problem was that Aloha Motors didn't have enough inventory to keep up with the orders. Dealerships that were not directly involved in the war were selling everything they could at discounts; there was an opportunity to buy low and sell high.

In 1943, Rich Grandfather called upon his network of associates—almost 600 truck dealers in total around the country—and bought 2,600 trucks by telephone. Grandfather stated in the *Forbes* magazine profile: "I got them all considerably under retail and often under cost." As the need for the war front became critical, Rich Grandfather would sell his trucks to Allied governments and list of contacts around the world.

As growth continued, Grandfather now needed a way to manage the system: the subject of the next chapter.

10

Step Eight: Manage The System

Right after the Second World War, Rich Grandfather was worth an estimated $2 million (as reported in the previously mentioned article in the *Melfort Journal*). Although $2 million was a long way from his dream of $100 million, it was still a lot of money to a farm boy. He then used the money from wartime profits to buy car dealerships in several locations around the United States, including a Chrysler-Dodge dealership in Omaha, Nebraska; a Chevrolet dealership in Los Angeles; dealerships in Oakland and Burbank, California; a Chevrolet dealership in Pasco, Washington; a Dodge dealership in Seattle; and the White Truck franchise in the state of Washington.

Rich Grandfather was on a roll, building momentum. He was on the fast track to accomplishing his goal of entering the N-business. By this time in his life, he had a firm grasp and understanding of his Aloha Money Machine. He understood his primary source of income; he understood his target customers and business story. He had leveraged his database and built a system around all of it. The only thing he had to do now was to find a way to manage multiple businesses at one time.

It's impressive how successful Rich Grandfather was at multiplying the Aloha Money Machine and repeating the process with consistent results, but he couldn't gain true success by merely creating a system; he now had to find a way to manage the system. Grandfather knew that he couldn't keep track of all his newly purchased dealerships without a way to manage them from a distance.

Once again, he needed to deconstruct the business like a mechanic deconstructs a machine. What were the tasks he couldn't delegate to others? After deconstructing his daily tasks, he found that there were two primary tasks he couldn't delegate. He found that he could manage multiple businesses from one location if he paid close attention to the money and culture of the business.

Money is the ultimate gauge to manage the system. It gives you real-time feedback, and it never lies. The P&L report is black-and-white. Either you're making money, and your business is thriving, or you're losing money, and your business needs help. There is no room for interpretation if your numbers and accounting are correct. You know what they say, figures never lie, but sometimes liars figure, so you have to pay close attention to the money.

Rich Grandfather understood that there was no such thing as a set-it-and-forget-it approach to the Aloha Money Machine. Although Grandfather could not possibly be at all of his businesses at the same time, he did watch the money and accounting of each business every day. Once the management system was in place, he could manage the success of his businesses by tracking the numbers. The financial figures were the heart of his business empire. Income and expenses directly determine the health of any business, and Rich Grandfather paid close attention to these.

One of the first employees Rich Grandfather hired was a bookkeeper. He understood the importance of knowing the numbers on a daily basis versus a yearly basis. Understanding his P&L statement helped him take advantage of critical information to make decisions on a moment's notice.

One formula that is commonly used in $100,000 to $2 million annual-revenue small businesses is the 50/30/20 formula. The formula is intended to allocate expenses after the cost of the sale is subtracted from gross revenues. The 50 translates to 50 percent of ODI (owner's discretionary income). This is what the owner takes home; the 30 means 30 percent dedicated to business development expenses; the remaining 20 represents 20 percent for office administration expenses. This is one road map for managing small business expenses. When setting a budget, it's important to note that your monthly budget is set before you spend the money. At the beginning of the month, determine how much you spend on office supplies, rent, salaries, food, utilities, and entertainment, then stick to your budget and don't spend more than allowed.

The key to managing the system is to *know your numbers* and *track your numbers*. Think about business in football terms. Tracking your income is like the offense, and tracking your expenses is like the defense. Just as in football, the business also has an offense and defense. To track your numbers, you must understand your offense (income) to determine where your income is coming from and if you're on target to reach your goals. In order to determine a successful financial goal, you must first determine your break-even amount. How much money do you need to make on a regular basis to cover your monthly expenses? The minimum amount to strive for is a break-even amount at which your income matches your expenses. But it's important to set a goal that is much higher than break-even.

Set a realistic financial goal by calculating your average sales over the last twelve months. Once you have this number, divide that number by twelve to determine your realistic monthly income goal. This is your benchmark number. But if you want to be rich, you need to set an *optimistic number* (a term borrowed from my own business coach, Mark LeBlanc).

An optimistic number is how much you would realistically like to make this year. If you want to make more money, you have to set bigger goals. To do this, set an optimistic goal: say $500,000 a year. Divide your optimistic yearly income goal of $500,000 by twelve months (500,000 ÷ 12 = $42,000 a month). To achieve your goal of $500,000 a year, you now know you need to make $42,000 a month. Now, based on what you sell, how many units (products) will you need to sell to make $42,000 a month?

Following the numbers on a monthly basis can provide early warning indications that are invaluable to the business. Knowing the numbers gives the business owner real-time feedback on the health of the business. It also offers time to react to negative (or positive) changes in the market. Knowing your numbers is the secret to managing the Aloha Money Machine for any size business. Keeping track of the numbers helps business owners increase profitability and make smarter decisions.

The Culture

Managing the system is much more than regulating the numbers, however; it is also maintaining the business culture. Rich Grandfather understood that the real product he sold was not his cars and trucks, but the *feeling* he gave his consumers when they bought a new car or truck from his dealerships. His true commodity was how the customers felt about his dealerships and the buying experience. The way the company interacted with its customers was more important than what it sold. That is why Rich Grandfather spent extra attention nurturing his employee culture, as he knew that his employees would be responsible for customer relationships.

Business culture is critical to the Aloha Money Machine. The owner's vision of the business, values, and reason why he or she created a company in the first place needs to be expressed to all employees. The business story needs to be repeated throughout the business. Business owners need to tell employees what problem the company solves and what passion the company has for solving the problem. The most profitable companies in the world help employees understand why they work for a company and how they make a difference in the work that they do.

Rich Grandfather also knew the only way people would stay in his business was if he had the right culture, which helped employee retention. Grandfather hired people who were like-minded and people whom he wanted to be around. He hired people who had fun in their free time but produced results when they were at work.

There is a custom in Hawaii called *Pau Hana* that Rich Grandfather supported. *Pau Hana* means "work is finished," and the term is used informally to mean celebrating the end of a workday. Generally on Fridays you will see groups of coworkers gathered together doing just that. *Pau Hana* is more than just a happy hour; it's a company's culture. It was important for Rich Grandfather to have a team of employees who had a philosophy of "working hard to play hard." If you didn't enjoy working hard (or *Pau Hana*), Rich Grandfather didn't want you on his team.

Although Rich Grandfather was a driver at work and expected a lot from his employees, he did treat his employees well. While Rich Grandfather had hundreds of employees, he still valued the individual people he hired and the culture that surrounded them.

Grandfather was able to manage several businesses and hundreds of employees because he controlled the culture of the business, not the individual person.

By the 1950s Rich Grandfather would expand his empire to a whole different level.

11

Step Nine: Highest And Best Use of Time

From his appearance, no one else in line at the Newark airport could know that the man standing next to them was worth $100 million. He looked like any other businessman, but if you watched closely, something was different about him. He had an air of confidence and a swagger in his step.

Although he had made millions in the past, he was at a whole different level now. Rich Grandfather thought it would be different at the top once he made $100 million, but it wasn't. He was the same man. He didn't feel different or feel the need to flaunt his money, show off, or be someone he wasn't. Although he was now confident in his financial situation, he still spoke in simple terms that people could understand. He wasn't trying to be something that he wasn't anymore; now he was officially a $100 millionaire.

Maybe that's why people liked him, and that's why he felt content flying commercial airlines. But another reason Rich Grandfather hadn't purchased his own jet yet was that he believed he traveled too much. Rich Grandfather was flying an average of 16,000 miles a week. That amount of air travel would require multiple airplanes and pilots to sustain.

Needless to say, shortly after completing a string of successful deals, he did buy three separate airplanes to accommodate his extensive travel. Later, he traded in the three planes for a luxury Learjet; the dependability and fuel efficiency were much better.

With continued success buying and selling dealerships, Rich Grandfather was at the top of his career. He was officially rich and had achieved his goal of entering the N-business (noble rich). More importantly, he was now respected for being rich. He had dreamed of this day, worked his whole life to get to this level, following his business compass. He had finally made it.

But for some reason, he still was not satisfied. Strangely, the taste of $100 million was not enough. He wanted more. He believed that if he could make $100 million, he could make $200 million. He now believed that if he had $200 million in the bank, then and only then would he be happy. Also, he felt he couldn't retire. He was still young and ready to take on the world. But the money had only brought him temporary happiness, and he was always in search of the next big score.

A Change In Direction

"After years of preaching that you should never get out of what you're good at, I got out of cars and trucks; I could see the writing on the wall after the war. Production was booming way ahead of sales. Overproduction was destroying a fine business. I had been getting more than a twelve percent return on my investments, and suddenly, I was getting two percent," Rich Grandfather said in the *Forbes* magazine interview.

Although Rich Grandfather kept Aloha Motors in Honolulu, he moved away from the rest of his dealerships and focused on buying and selling other types of businesses. He felt the best use of his time was now selling big-ticket items. Millions could be made in one deal, versus hundreds or thousands selling vehicles. The previously referenced 2008 article in the *Regina Leader-Post* quotes a 1968 article in *The Wall Street Journal* where Rich Grandfather explained, "I buy rundown, poor-management companies, analyze them, then come in and clean house." He would use his Aloha Money Machine Method to "clean house," in his words.

Rich Grandfather would learn:

Growing your business into a salable business is what you need to do to experience financial freedom. Once you do this, you can then sell the business and experience what it is like to be rich.

Rich Grandfather knew that the only way he could achieve his new goal of earning $200 million would be to buy and sell businesses full-time. He would change his title from business owner to Investor. He knew that he could achieve his goal if he made the connections and networked with people who bought and sold multimillion-dollar businesses. He would now pursue the highest and best use of his time by networking with the super-rich.

As Rich Grandfather made the transition from auto dealer to business tycoon, he had a difficult time once again convincing the super-rich he was a good investment. Although he'd had success in the auto dealership industry, he was operating at a whole different level now. But as time went by, his contact list grew, and he established himself as a successful buyer and seller of businesses among the rich.

Rich Grandfather was now becoming recognized as an authority on buying and selling businesses. Due to this recognition, people sought him out for advice. He suddenly had opportunities that had once been impossible to find. Instead of seeking business, he was attracting it, and he made a commitment to honoring his highest and best use of time.

The best example that I found of Rich Grandfather's commitment to his highest and best use of time was an article in *Hawaii Weekly* published in 1965. Rich Grandfather was recognized as a United Airlines Million-Miler club member; the club was formed to honor the few people who had flown more than a million miles. (A million miles is the equivalent distance of forty-plus times around the world.)

From the aforementioned article in the *Regina Leader-Post*: "'He spends half his time flying in pursuit of his fortunes,' said his brother Graydon Murphy. 'His hobby is making money—and buying up corporations.'"

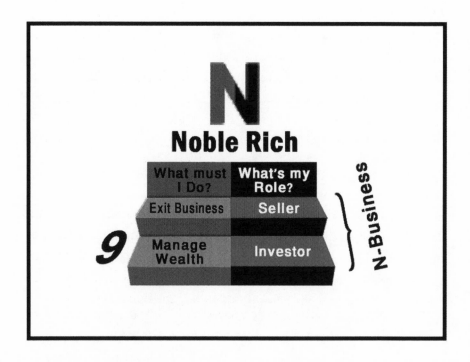

As you can imagine, Rich Grandfather's time was precious. But he believed that his time was best used meeting buyers and sellers face-to-face. Because of this belief, he traveled approximately 46,000 air miles per month and committed most of his life to this belief.

The Rich Becomes Ultrarich

By the 1950s and 1960s, Rich Grandfather had expanded into such diverse companies as manufacturing appliances, tools, industrial equipment, oil, pineapples, ranching, ironworks, and even real estate.

My dad remembers getting a phone call in the middle of the night. The phone call was from Rich Grandfather, who was overseas and oblivious to the fact that it was 1:00 a.m. in Hawaii.

"Hello," Rich Grandfather said, "I just sold Honolulu Iron Works for $15 million. Tell the rest of the family. I have to go now." And he hung up the phone. The conversation ended quickly without even a word from my dad. This was Rich Grandfather's style: He came in fast and left just as fast; he didn't have time for small talk or pleasantries. My dad knew that this was a big deal, as Rich Grandfather didn't usually make phone calls to the family on small $1 million or $2 million deals.

I would find out later that Rich Grandfather sold Honolulu Iron Works for $15 million, which he had bought three years earlier for $4 million.

Although Rich Grandfather may have been extraordinarily successful as a buyer and seller of companies, he still considered himself to be nothing more than a simple "horse trader who has diversified [quoting from the aforementioned *Forbes* interview]." Granted, he was turning sway-backed old plugs into thoroughbreds, but still a simple horse trader who diversified.

Halawa Valley, Pu'u O Hoku Ranch, Molokai

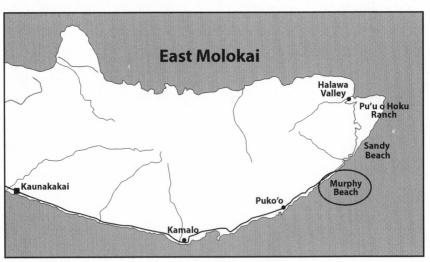

Murphy Beach located on the east end of Molokai.

In 1955, Rich Grandfather bought 14,000 acres of Pu'u O Hoku Ranch on the island of Molokai in Hawaii. Although his plan was to cultivate his expanding network of business associates by entertaining them on the Molokai ranch, his life-long goal was to be a successful rancher. His goal was to turn the ranch into a real working ranch and to be the first person to import purebred Charolais cattle from France to Hawaii.

While Rich Grandfather would find relaxation in the cattle business, he still applied the same drive and demands he expected from his other employees to the ranch hands. One of the ranch hands included was my dad, who was responsible for tending to the cattle as a *poniolo* (Hawaiian name for cowboy).

In exchange for work, Rich Grandfather allowed my dad and mom to live in a small beach home on the ranch. Although the beach home was small, it was in a great location directly across the street from Murphy Beach. Murphy Beach, characteristically named after Rich Grandfather, is a narrow, white-sand beach lined with palm trees that still remains on Molokai today. The small beach home included an outside shower, outside kitchen, and a horse corral in the front yard. I would spend the first three years of my life in this home before moving to the mainland.

Rich Grandfather expanded the Pu'u O Hoku Ranch and constructed a hunting lodge with ten bedrooms and twelve bathrooms. The lodge featured panoramic views of the rugged coastal bluffs overlooking the blue Pacific Ocean. Below the lodge, he constructed a private airport to accommodate his Learjet and guests' airplanes.

Although he considered the ranch a "money-making hobby," his real motivation was to build relationships with his database of business associates. Rich Grandfather knew building relationships with these people would ultimately help him accomplish his new goal of earning $200 million. The lodge also offered his guests hunting opportunities with year-round deer, wild boar, pheasant, and quail in abundance.

Although Rich Grandfather did complete his goal, importing Charolais cattle into Hawaii, his big dreams of becoming a successful rancher never came to reality. The ranch never made the kind of money that impressed ultrarich Texas oil tycoons, but it did give him something much more than money. It gave him an opportunity to build relationships with some of the most affluent people in the world.

Rich Grandfather would spend much time in airplanes in the 1960s, traveling from his Molokai ranch to his business interests in Los Angeles, San Francisco, Seattle, Kansas City, Houston, Chicago, New York, and Australia.

As Rich Grandfather's financial career skyrocketed, he now had the money and credibility to buy large companies. One of those companies was the car manufacturer Studebaker. For fifty years during the twentieth century, Studebaker was a large and successful auto manufacturing company in America, but as times would have it, the company ran into financial problems and needed help. Rich Grandfather saw an opportunity to turn this once-giant company around and pursued buying it. In the mid-1960s, Rich Grandfather's plan was to use the $15 million from the sale of Honolulu Iron Works, to buy Studebaker for $3.6 million.

But the Studebaker deal didn't go through. Studebaker announced in March 1966 that it would no longer make cars. One can only imagine what might have happened to Studebaker if Rich Grandfather had been successful in taking over the company and turning it around as he had so many other companies.

In the 1967 *Forbes* interview, Rich Grandfather said his work was so stimulating that he "couldn't do anything else. I've worked twenty hours a day, seven days a week, for the past thirty years." During this time, the family barely saw Rich Grandfather, as his full-time pursuit of fortune consumed him.

At the height of his career, Rich Grandfather was now worth an estimated $500 million. He would surpass his goal of $200 million by more than double. Although he would accomplish his goal many times over. Rich Grandfather would never find the happiness he was looking for, no pot of gold at the end of the rainbow.

The previously referenced 2008 article from the *Leader-Post* summarized Rich Grandfather's final years. Late in life, Rich Grandfather sold off virtually all his business interests, including his pride and joy, Aloha Motors in Honolulu. He sold off the Molokai Ranch, his construction business, his manufacturing business, his real estate business, and his steel business. The article says, "None of his family or grandchildren continued in his businesses or dealerships. George Murphy died at his home in Honolulu on November 22, 1989, at the age of 85, ending a remarkable life in which a farm boy had gone on to own the largest General Motors dealership in the world."

PART III

Selling the Aloha Money Machine

The Next Step

It is said that Michelangelo saw the statue of David in the huge chunk of raw marble before he ever started working on his sculpture. Some say Michelangelo was successful because he could see the end before he began. This vision allowed him to create one of the most famous statues in the world.

Having a clear vision of building a business that could be sold from the start, even if he had no intention of selling, helped Rich Grandfather achieve his goal many times over.

I, too, found that same philosophy—building a salable business from the very start—would help me achieve my goal of becoming successful through business.

After ten years of operating, I was now contemplating the idea of selling my own business. But I, like Rich Grandfather, was hesitant to sell, as my cash flow was now stable and my system was strong. Although I was hesitant, I knew that if the system was strong enough, I could start another business. Maybe this time, I would expand my business across the world (either around the world or across the globe) and use technology as my platform.

The best part about building your own Aloha Money Machine is that it will give you options, and options give you leverage. With leverage, you have power, and the possibilities of what you could do with your business are endless.

With a nod to *Built to Sell*, here are a few examples of what business owners can do once they have created their own Aloha Money Machine:[12]

1. You can sell the business for a profit and use the earnings for retirement, investing in a new company, or giving a portion of the profit to charity. Bill and Melinda Gates give away billions by way of their foundation. Although there are many things you can do with the profit, I suggest that you have a detailed plan in place for your future after the sale. How do you see your life once you sell your business? What will you do with your extra time once the business is sold? Many business owners will find themselves relieved once the business is sold, but after the romance of selling a business disappears, many of these same business owners will find themselves searching for their next step. The four biggest questions that you should ask before selling are: Where will you spend your money? Where will you spend your time? What will give you purpose and happiness? How will you track your success without business income? Some business owners will struggle to find purpose in their lives. When they owned a business, the business gave them a reason to wake up every day. Without the business, many post-exit owners struggle to find a way to track success, as money is the ultimate measurement of success. The trick to selling a business is to have a clear vision of what life will look like after you sell. What new activities and goals will give your life purpose, and how will you track those? With whom will you associate, how will you pay your bills, what expenses will you have, where will you volunteer your time, and what will give

---

[12] John Warrillow, *Built to Sell: Creating a Business That Can Thrive without You* (New York: Portfolio/Penguin, 2012).

you joy? Do you want to continue your business career, or do you want to collect a return on your investment and retire? These are the decisions you must make *before* you sell the business.

2. You can gift the business to employees or family. Some of the most significant companies in the world are ultimately gifted to employees or family. There are tax advantages to this method of business exit; you will not have to pay a large amount in capital gains. (Please know I'm not a tax advisor or certified financial planner and I'm not qualified to advise you on these issues. Seek the guidance of a certified professional.) Many people take this approach and require that the qualified family member pay a lump sum or make the monthly payment on a regular basis to the seller.

3. You can expand the business. If you decide to grow the business, you must build a scalable business. "Scalability is one of the most critical factors for entrepreneurs…hoping to take a current business to the next level. Successful business growth depends on a scalable business model that will increase profits over time by growing revenue while avoiding cost increases."[13] Scalability describes the capability to perform well under an expanding scope. A system that scales well can maintain performance as it gets larger. Financially speaking, a scalable company is one that can keep or grow profit margins while revenues increase.

4. You can trade your business for a new business. Rich Grandfather loved this approach. He would trade businesses to capitalize on his current resources. Taking the game of Monopoly, for example, in which two little green houses are traded for a big red hotel, Rich Grandfather would trade businesses that leveraged other businesses he owned. In some situations, he would trade businesses and leverage

---

[13] Will Housh, "Choosing a Business Model That Will Grow Your Company," *Entrepreneur*, March 12, 2015, https://www.entrepreneur.com/article/243237, Accessed August 29, 2019.

his auto dealerships to supply the transportation he needed for the new business he had just acquired.

5. You can borrow against the business. Similar to a home equity line of credit, you can borrow against the equity in the business and use the money to pay off debt or invest in a new opportunity. Banks love loaning money to successful companies, but you must make sure you do not overextend yourself.

6. You can franchise the business. If your Aloha Money Machine system is strong enough, you can franchise the system, trademark the name, and sell it to potential franchise buyers, as McDonald's does with restaurants. Although, at it's core, McDonald's is not really in the hamburger business—they are in the real estate business, as was my Rich Grandfather. McDonald's just happens to operate fast food restaurants built on their real estate. "You want capital gains with that?"

7. You can sell off portions of the business. Rich Grandfather was very creative when buying and selling businesses. He looked at the many aspects of a company to figure out what portions of the business could be separated. In many cases, he bought businesses that owned real estate and separated the real estate from the business into two separate corporations. He then sold the business and kept the real estate on which the business operated. In some situations, he sold a business with the contractual agreement that the buyer pays him monthly lease payments for the life of the business after it was sold. Rich Grandfather also *loved* buying real estate that a business operated on as it limited his risks. His idea was to have the business pay for the real estate, and if the business failed, he would still own the real estate.

To those of you who have successfully built your own form of The Aloha Money Machine and are now looking to take the next step,

I congratulate you. You have accomplished something only a small percentage of business owners will achieve. For many of us, the next step will be the biggest decision you will make. Some will need help on the direction of their next step; others will need help understanding the best place to put their cash once they sell the business.

The Tragic End Of Rich Grandfather

While Rich Grandfather's story sounds like a classic, underdog, rags-to-riches tale, I believe his life was really a tragedy, a rags-to-riches-to-rags-to-riches-to rags story. His tragic flaw was that he put money over everything else. Ultimately, he was not willing to create a legacy by sharing his knowledge with others. Ultimately, his legacy of business died with him and his knowledge of wealth withered away as he was unwilling to physically share his knowledge with others.

Before I could decide on what to do with my own business, I believed that I needed to know Rich Grandfather's decision-making process on selling his own businesses. I needed to know why Rich Grandfather sold some businesses and kept others, and I still wanted to uncover the mystery of how Rich Grandfather lost all his money at the end of his life.

To understand Rich Grandfather's mindset, I thought it would be best to ask the person who knew him best. Once again, I would seek the advice of my dad to uncover the mystery of my Rich Grandfather.

Throughout the years, I had heard stories of how Rich Grandfather made millions in business, but I didn't understand why my dad had never pursued the family business. Maybe if I could understand this, I would understand the reason why Rich Grandfather lost all his money and why he sold some businesses but kept others.

Thinking of these questions, I became frustrated. Why did I have to work so hard to grow my own business, and why did I have to struggle when my dad could have just inherited the family business? I didn't understand why we had to start from scratch when Rich Grandfather could have offered my dad a business to run. Maybe this was the reason Rich Grandfather had lost all his money at the end of his life. Maybe he'd had no one to take over his businesses. Perhaps I should keep my business and give it to my future children, I thought. I didn't want to make the same mistakes as Rich Grandfather. I needed answers, and I needed to hear them from my dad, in person.

I booked a flight from San Diego to Hawaii and arranged to meet my dad and talk. Once I landed in Hawaii, I rented a car and drove to my family's house in Kailua-Kona, Hawaii. My dad immediately saw the frustration on my face and asked what was wrong.

"I need to ask you a few questions about the non-existent family business," I said.

I remember my dad took a deep breath and asked me to sit down. He looked me right in the eyes and said, "Rich Grandfather was one of the best salesmen that you ever met. As a kid, I believed everything he said. His stories were amazing. His riches were inspiring.

"However, with time, I began to see the holes in the stories, and the truth showed itself. I think Rich Grandfather excelled at buying and selling businesses because he was a master at storytelling. He was a master at his business story and the short game. He told people what they wanted to hear and what they needed to hear. But in the long game, he failed, and his family called bullshit.

"Because of this, it made it very difficult for me to believe him or trust him. In fact, it made it difficult for me to believe *anyone* in sales," Dad said. "I saw firsthand what a truly talented salesman was capable of doing and what he could do to a family. Rich Grandfather was always selling himself to the family; he was always selling in general. I genuinely don't think he could stop. Selling, in general, is not a bad thing. Everyone sells themselves in one way or another. If you meet someone new, you must sell yourself if you desire a relationship with that person.

"You must smile, say hello, or seem interested if you want to make friends. However, things take a turn for the worst when you start selling ideas and values that you don't believe in *yourself*.

"Rich Grandfather made it clear that he was willing to do *anything* and say anything to get what he wanted, and his family was not excluded. Once you bring sales tactics home and start selling your family on ideas that you don't believe yourself, you start breaking the trust of the family," Dad said.

"Once you ruin your family's trust, a sacred family bond is broken."

Because of this, my dad never pursued the family business. He thought all salesmen were the same and he didn't want to do that to his own family. He believed it was just a matter of time before all salespeople bring "the bullshit" home. He simply didn't want to be a part of a cycle that had hurt his family.

In that moment I felt an overwhelming appreciation for my Dad's commitment to stand up for what he believed. I appreciated the fact that my dad took a stand for what he believed and didn't follow the footsteps of monetary greed. I also appreciated the hard work my Dad endured building his own successful business and providing for his family by his own means.

In the end, Rich Grandfather's greed for money eventually got the best of him and broke the family trust beyond repair. At the end of his life, it was clear that Rich Grandfather would do or say anything for money. He was willing to burn down the city, including his children's home, to make more money. No one was excluded. He was never satisfied or happy with his financial situation. He always wanted more. Rich Grandfather eventually broke the sacred family bond, and the family would never recover.

From that day forward, Rich Grandfather never made it back to the titan businessman he once had been. He would never rejoin the ranks of the noble-rich, and his health would quickly be diminished. He was no longer the influential Hawaii business leader who bought and sold multimillion-dollar companies. Seemingly overnight, he became a frail man who second-guessed himself and was unable to keep score of his businesses as he once had with ease.

But the worst part about Rich Grandfather's greed was that he thought money would eventually bring him happiness. Having once tasted success, he had arrogance and an ego that would not let him admit to weakness. He held himself in high regard, without empathy, even though he hurt many people. Because he was embarrassed and couldn't admit that he was wrong for choosing money over people, he died a lonely man, unable to trust.

There is a difference between rich families and poor families other than the size of their bank accounts. The real difference has nothing to do with money and everything to do with knowledge.

The knowledge of how to make money, how to multiply money, how to grow money, and how to protect the money is the real power behind wealth. Without this shared knowledge passed down from generation to generation, or the knowledge learned from others, the secret of wealth dies and does not live on. Ultimately, the philosophy of scarcity and greed repeats itself, and the poor remain poor.

There is a time in everyone's life when we will be unable to take care of ourselves. We will be too old to manage our finances. We will be too old to do housework. We will be too old to make money. In most people's lives, this is the time when the family gets involved and takes away the car, cleans out the house of unused items, clears out projects they will never get around to, and eventually loved ones hold their hands to the end of their lives.

Being a witness to my aging grandparents, I realized that this applies to all business owners as well. I understood that there is a time in all business owners' lives when they must walk away from the business. For some of us, the reason we must step away is that we are too old and simply don't have the energy or mental capabilities to keep track of our affairs. For others, it might be a business partner disagreement or the business owner is burnt out, or there is a new opportunity to pursue. No matter what the reason, we all must walk away from our businesses someday. Either you will make the decision, or life will decide for you, but the day will come for all of us.

People ask me all the time, "But how did Rich Grandfather lose all his money? How could he acquire so many riches in such a short time and lose it all?"

Rich Grandfather eventually reached a level at which he was too old to manage his businesses and needed help. The problem was, he had burned many bridges, and had very few people left around him whom he could trust. His family didn't trust him because of his dishonesty, and he didn't trust his family because of his guilt.

He had no one to trust or rely on, so he turned to the only people he could, and that was his lawyers. His lawyers were no different from Rich Grandfather; they, too, were out for blood and would do anything for money. The day Rich Grandfather asked his lawyers to control his money was the day he lost control.

The lawyers saw it as an opportunity to capitalize on Rich Grandfather's weakness. These people were longtime associates who had witnessed firsthand the lack of trust Rich Grandfather showed his business partners and family at the end of his career. They would eventually show no mercy as well.

Once others took control, it was like a feeding frenzy. Everyone wanted a piece. Every parasite and vulture were scraping and pulling raw meat off the bones of Rich Grandfather's businesses. Because of the lack of trust and trusting the wrong people, Rich Grandfather would eventually lose his money.

The beauty of creating the Aloha Money Machine is that it doesn't matter what you intend to do with the business as long as you know your *why*. *Why* will be the most critical question that you ask yourself. Why would you want to sell your business? Why would you want to expand or franchise your business? Why do you want to take your business in a new direction? Rich Grandfather's *Why* was to make money. His goal was to make $100 million. Once he made $100 million, he then wanted to make $200 million. It didn't matter how much money Rich Grandfather made; he was never satisfied. Rich Grandfather would find out that his lifelong goal to make money would only buy him temporary fulfillment. Unfortunately, his business compass was set in a direction of temporary achievement through money, and ultimately, he would die a lonely man, run aground on the rocky shores of bankruptcy.

I saw the writing on the wall, and I was not going to make the same mistake.

After talking with my dad, I knew that I did not want to take the same path as Rich Grandfather and follow money exclusively. I wanted my family to love me, I wanted to leave a legacy, and most importantly, I wanted to live a life that made a positive difference to others. Also, I knew that the only way that my business would grow to the next level is if I expanded to another city. My business already had a large percentage of the market share in San Diego. I had grown my business as far as I could in my area. There were only so many people who owned wood patio furniture, and if I wanted to continue my growth, I would need to expand to a different city.

Because I wasn't interested in following the path of money exclusively, and I wasn't interested in developing my business to a different city, I decided to sell. I would sell my Aloha Money Machine and focus on building a life of purpose, full of legacy.

But after my decision to sell, I had a problem. It would be months of waiting for someone to respond to my free Craigslist.org ad listing my business for sale. I had no offers and I had no phone calls from potential buyers. Although Rich Grandfather had fallen short of leaving a legacy, I still admired him for his business experiences and would look to him for guidance one last time.

I needed to research how he had sold businesses.

I was curious why it was so easy for him and why I was having such a hard time. I had always thought it would be easy to sell my business once I had built the Aloha Money Machine, but it wasn't. I had created a salable business just like Rich Grandfather would have himself. So, why was I having such a hard time selling it?

I realized the reason Rich Grandfather was able to buy and sell businesses so quickly was that he associated and networked with people who bought businesses. He networked with wealthy We-business owners daily, and I was associating with the S-business owners. If I wanted to sell my business, I needed to make a change and get in front of the right people: those who had the cash and resources to buy a profitable business.

I did precisely that. I researched and located my target customers. I analyzed my target audience to find out what buyers of businesses wanted. I created my business story and advertised a teaser description of the business to a network of people who had the funds and means to buy businesses. I organized my system in an easy-to-understand document called *The Book*. The book was a complete description of the business that included a future plan for business growth. Learn from the past, live in the present, plan for the end.

Once *The Book* was completed, I next prepared my employees for the sale. I understood that a smart buyer would want to meet employees before the sale and make agreements, so key employees were prepared.

Although it was difficult to tell my employees that I was selling the business and the fear that they would leave was stressful, I found it was actually easier than expected. Employees were excited for new opportunities to grow with the company. (I also found that Rich Grandfather had this same fear. His solution to keeping employees during the sale of a business was never to offer stock options because this was too messy. Rather, he offered his employees cash bonuses for continuing their employment throughout the sale of the business.) Once my business was prepared for the sale, I used the highest and best use of my time to network with my target audience of buyers, and eventually, I sold my business for a profit.

At thirty-one years old, I officially became a millionaire. I collected 83 percent of the sale in cash and carried a note for the remaining 17 percent of the business. The buyer would pay me 8 percent interest on a private loan for the next five years.

Although I would like to say I knew what it meant to build a meaningful life full of legacy after I sold my business, I didn't. I would spend the next eight years finding the answers to what that looked like. I came to find out that the secret to living a meaningful life would require building two more companies.

The first company that I would need to build would be the Aloha Lending Machine. Although I had a chunk of money from the sale of my business, I didn't have a regular income to cover my ongoing bills. I needed to develop a new system that leveraged the money to pay for my living expenses. I needed a way to make my money last, and I needed a way to make money from my money. To accomplish this, I built the Aloha Lending Machine, investing in cash flow real estate and private loans. Once I created the Aloha Lending Machine to stabilize my income from a steady flow of rentals and private loans, I then used my time to build a meaningful life full of legacy. To do this, I built my third business: the Aloha Legacy Machine.

The Secret Of Fulfillment After You Sell

Let me leave you with a closing thought. After I sold my business, I was looking for the next step. Now that I had money, what should my purpose be? I found that money is not fulfillment, but sharing the knowledge of how to make money *did* bring fulfillment. The secret to fulfillment after you have created your Aloha Money Machine is to share your knowledge with others and to leave a legacy. If you help others make money, you can create the most positive impact. That is what I want to explore with you in the epilogue.

EPILOGUE

Aloha's Secret Weapon: Becoming Noble-Rich

Consider Uber, which I believe to be a noble business model. Many people believe that the success of Uber is a result of the company creating a better taxi service—that the experience is more efficient, or the drivers are more courteous, or the response time is quicker.

But the reality is that the simple act of picking someone up and driving them to their destination is not something new or different. Uber did not reinvent the wheel, no matter how you slice it; it is still a taxi service.

So why is Uber changing the world as we know it? How is it that a ten-year-old taxi service that doesn't own a single car is now worth $80 billion, while Ford, a 100-year-old company, is worth just $40 billion?

Because Uber is giving *many* people ways to make money, and Ford does not.

The real advantage of Uber is that Uber gives ordinary people an opportunity to become S-business owners and make money for themselves. It provides people with no more than a car and a drivers license the tools to enter the S-business economy. It gives people the chance to set their own hours and schedules to earn cash. Some people subsidize their incomes by driving a few hours with Uber; others use Uber as their primary source of income.

Uber has literally changed the world because it has adopted an Aloha-Money-Machine-like philosophy. Uber is successful because it helps others become successful. And that is noble.

Time To Consider A Noble Business

This epilogue is designed to show you a new definition for noble and how to build a noble business that changes the world.

Many business owners decide to go into business for themselves, as they want to make a difference, and they want to change the world. These people are motivated by more than money. They are motivated that their product or service will make a difference in people's lives. They risk everything and invest their lives and money into opening a business. They spend their time, energy, blood, sweat, and tears. They sacrifice time with family, spouses, and even their children to grow a business that makes a difference. These hardcore business owners want to leave a legacy and to be remembered for making a difference in this world. Many of these business owners, however, will fail.

The secret weapon behind the Aloha Money Machine is the same secret that makes Hawaii great. The meaning of *aloha* goes beyond any definition you can find in dictionaries. The word *aloha* has several definitions. It does, in fact, mean hello and goodbye, but the real definition implies something much greater. *Aloha* is the greatest strength Hawaii has. Its power does not come from the military stationed in Hawaii. It does not come from agriculture, big wave surfing, Hawaii's MMA fighting, or tourism. Its real strength comes from its people—the people of Hawaii who inhabit the islands and spread the *aloha* are Hawaii's real strength.

The melting pot of people who have traveled across the world to call Hawaii their home is the real power of Hawaii. Hawaii has taken the best of the best from Polynesian, Japan, the Philippines, Alaska, Europe, Samoa, and the United States. This melting pot has created something special called the Aloha Spirit.

The true definition of *aloha* is not about what you can get; it's about what you can give. *Aloha* is not about taking; it's about giving. *Aloha*, in its purest form, is about sacrifice. It's about caring, and it's about giving to someone else. *Aloha* is about having someone's best interest as a priority and loving your neighbor as yourself.

It might sound strange and goes against everything you've heard about business, but the power behind the Aloha Money Machine and building a business that changes the world is that it's not about making money for yourself; it's about making money for others. The power of aloha is: it's not about you.

The Secrets Of Businesses That Change The World

How do you build a business that changes the world? The answer is by creating a company that helps business owners get what they want. All business owners want a way to make money and be in control of their own time. Although the success of Uber was a mixture of technology and philosophy, the philosophy of Uber was the cornerstone of their success.

Likewise, the Aloha Money Machine philosophy is not a new concept. It has been around forever.

If you look throughout history, you will see the Aloha Money Machine philosophy has been living among us since the beginning of time.

---

*Helping others become successful in gaining
personal success is not a new concept.*

If you look throughout history, you will see this example repeatedly.

Middle Ages. In the middle ages, it wasn't the merchants in villages who made the biggest difference; it was the business owners who constructed the toll roads and bridges to the villages who made the biggest difference.

Industrial Age. In the industrial age, it wasn't the manufacturers who built machines who became truly wealthy; it was the manufacturers of coal and oil that fueled the machines who became truly wealthy.

Gold Rush Age. The people who made the most money in the California gold rush were not the miners or prospectors digging for gold. The people who made the most money were the merchants who sold shovels, picks, and pants to the miners.

During Wartime. In times of war, it wasn't governments that got rich; it was the people who were selling arms, clothing, and vehicles (like my Rich Grandfather in WWII) that got rich.

Digital Age. In the digital age, Bill Gates (for example) of Microsoft didn't become one of the wealthiest people in the world because he built computers. He became one of the wealthiest people in the world because he built the software running the computers to help business owners become successful.

What This Means For Today

You can get everything in life you want if you will just help enough other people get what they want.

—Zig Ziglar

My main message is this: Give people what they want to be successful in business, and you will be successful yourself. The people who become rich in life are the people who help others become rich. This is the true definition of noble-rich.

S-business revolution is stronger now than ever before. With companies like Uber, Airbnb, and Etsy, it is now easier than ever to start your own S-business. Millions of business owners are selling merchandise every day online. But the majority of people getting rich are not the ones selling merchandise. Instead, those getting rich are the ones *helping* these people sell their merchandise online, like Amazon and eBay.

Amazon.com, for example, is a cloud-based business that helps business owners sell merchandise online and has experienced growth of more than 50 percent every year since 2006. This company is experiencing massive growth because it is providing a platform for S-business owners to sell their products online and ultimately make money. Amazon is successful because it is helping others become successful. In turn, Amazon is changing the world.

Rich Grandfather dreamed of the day he would enter the ranks of the noble-rich. As he looked at his business compass as a poor boy living on his parents' farm, the goal of achieving noble-rich status was an incredible dream. He believed that if he were able to make it into the class of the noble-rich, all his dreams would come true and he would be happy.

But once he reached his noble-rich definition, he was not satisfied. He would find out at the end of his life that the goal of making money exclusively was a hollow dream. The gratification of making money was quickly lost once the deal was complete. Rich Grandfather would find out at the end of his life that he was no longer achieving a dream; he was only feeding an addiction. Just like a drug addiction, he always wanted more, and more was never enough.

Because of this, Rich Grandfather fell short of reaching his full potential. If he simply changed his philosophy from self-serving to self-sacrifice, he could have really made a difference and possibly changed the world.

The noble-rich, the ones who help others become successful, are no longer the big auto manufacturers, the big banks, and the big oil companies. The noble-rich are now the Ubers of the world, the Amazons of the world, and the Airbnbs of the world, helping others become successful.

Give people what they want to be successful in business, and you will be successful yourself.

To be successful in business will take everything you have, and it won't be easy. It might seem at times that no one understands the challenges and struggles that you face. However, know that you are not alone; many have come before you and have faced the same problems and struggles that you face today.

As a business owner I, too, have felt alone. I didn't know where to turn for guidance. I believed that I had to do everything myself, but I have learned that business is a team sport. Reach out to people who have started a business, grown a business, and sold a business, and you will accomplish more in a shorter time.

Focus on the big picture of the business; where do you see the business when it's time to exit? If you know the direction of that, you can craft a model that drives you. If you craft a business model that encourages you, you can inspire others, give customers what they want, create loyalty, and surround yourself with people who want you to achieve your goal.

Those goals are possible. If you are willing to put in the work and manage your system on a regular basis, then anything is possible. Who knows? You might even change the world for the better. I wish you the best.

Aloha.

Afterword

As some might mistake George W. Murphy of Honolulu, Hawaii's Businessman of the Year, as being related to Robert Kiyosaki, author of the book *Rich Dad, Poor Dad,* I want to clarify here that he was not. My great grandfather, George W. Murphy, the main character in the *Aloha Money Machine,* was a real man who grew up poor and built his fortune in Hawaii. He was not the same person or intended to be the same person as Robert Kiyosaki's Rich Dad of Hawaii. The stories of George W. Murphy are based on true life and events of a real

Photo courtesy of Hawaii Business Magazine, *January 1965. George Murphy was named Hawaii's "Businessman of the Year" in 1965.*

man who lived and worked in Hawaii. This book reflects the author's present recollection of personal experiences over time. While this book is based on true stories, some names and characteristics have been changed; some events have been compressed, and some dialogue has been recreated.

APPENDIX A
Acknowledgments

It's crazy to think a person with dyslexia would want to write a book. For this reason I have a feeling that God had a serious hand in this. For this I thank you! I would also like to dedicate this book to my dad, George, who has always been my rock and cheerleader. To my mother, Donna, who has shown me the gift of sacrifice and giving. To my wife, Danielle, who has supported me when writing this book and encouraged me to be the best I can be. To my children, Merrick and Makai, who have given me my life's purpose and legacy. To my stepdad, Steve Hersh, who has shown me that anything is possible in business. To my mom, Denice, who has loved me unconditionally. To Scott Leonhard, who has motivated me to do big things. To George W. Murphy (Rich Grandfather), who has given me a formula to grow my own business. To my grandfather, Jim Deuling, who has shown me the secret to leaving a legacy. To my *Kailua-Kona Ohana,* who accepted me and showed me *aloha* from day one. To my San Diego *Ohana,* who have given me access to a world that most small-town island boys will never experience. To the band Pepper, who inspires me to keep *aloha* in my heart. To my editor Henry DeVries, of Indie Books International. To Shelia Wasson and people who have supported me on my journey to becoming an author. To Toastmasters Expressions Unlimited, who have given me the confidence to be a professional speaker. To all the people whom I have left out, but who have supported me and have shown me *aloha* throughout the years: Much love and Aloha.

APPENDIX B
About The Author

Corey "Murf" Murphy was born and raised in Hawaii and is a small business success story. He has owned and operated seven different businesses in his lifetime, including manufacturing, service, wholesale, online, import, retail, and real estate businesses. Since successfully selling his service business and becoming financially free at thirty-one years old he has had a passion to teach others his formula called the Aloha Money Machine. As a professional speaker, he speaks on growing business for profit, sales, real estate investing and growing businesses to sell.

Murf currently resides in San Diego, California with his beautiful wife Danielle and two children Merrick and Makai.

To contact Murf to purchase multiple copies of this book or to book Murf as a speaker (or invite him to a Luau), you may e-mail him at murf@alohamoneymachine.com, murfspeaks@gmail.com, or call him at 760-456-5333.

Works Referenced

Bowers, Brent. "Study shows stronger links between entrepreneurs and dyslexia," *The New York Times*, November 5, 2007. https://www.nytimes.com/2007/12/05/business/worldbusiness/05iht-dyslexia.4.8602036.html. Accessed August 21, 2019.

"Cold War Foreign Policy." Stanford History Education Group. https://sheg.stanford.edu/history-assessments/cold-war-foreign-policy.

"Former Melfort...Murphy Motors Organised; Major Step in Auto Field." *Melfort Journal*, July 12, 1938.

Gerber, Michael E. *The E-Myth: Why Most Small Businesses Don't Work and What to Do about It*. New York: HarperBusiness, 2001.

"Hawaii After Pearl Harbor." Visit Pearl Harbor, March 8, 2017. https://visitpearlharbor.org/hawaii-pearl-harbor/.

"Honolulu Horse Trader." *Forbes* magazine, July 1967.

Honolulu Star-Bulletin. July 23, 1939.

Housh, Will. "Choosing a Business Model That Will Grow Your Company." Entrepreneur, March 12, 2015. https://www.entrepreneur.com/article/243237, Accessed August 29, 2019.

Investopedia.com, Recurring Revenue page. https://www.investopedia.com/terms/r/recurringrevenue.asp. Accessed August 21, 2019.

Johnson, Dale. "GM's Biggest Dealer - From Saskatchewan." *Regina Leader-Post*. July 24, 2008.

McIntyre, Georgia. "What Percentage of Small Businesses Fail? (And Other Need-to-Know Stats)" Fundera.com, June 21, 2019. https://www.fundera.com/blog/what-percentage-of-small-businesses-fail. Article shares statistics from the U.S. Bureau of Labor Statistics Business Employment Dynamics report found here: https://www.bls.gov/bdm/us_age_naics_00_table7.txt. Accessed August 29, 2019.

Patrick, Josh. "Why Many Small Businesses Cannot Be Sold," You're The Boss blog, *The New York Times*, September 4, 2014. https://boss.blogs.nytimes.com/2014/09/04/why-many-small-businesses-cannot-be-sold/. Accessed August 29, 2019.

Warrillow, John. *Built to Sell: Creating a Business That Can Thrive Without You*. New York: Portfolio/Penguin, 2012.

Made in the USA
Monee, IL
05 February 2020